Handbuilt
Tableware

Handbuilt Tableware

MAKING DISTINCTIVE PLATES, BOWLS, MUGS, TEAPOTS, AND MORE

Kathy Triplett

LARK BOOKS

A DIVISION OF STERLING PUBLISHING CO., INC.
NEW YORK

Editor: Paige Gilchrist
Art Director and Production: Celia Naranjo
Photography: Dwayne Shell, Photographic Solutions
Assistant Editors: Veronika Alice Gunter, Heather Smith
Production Assistance: Hannes Charen

Library of Congress Cataloging-in-Publication Data

Triplett, Kathy, 1949-
    Handbuilt tableware : making distinctive plates, bowls, mugs, teapots, and more / Kathy Triplett.
       p. cm.
    Includes index.
    ISBN 1-57990-204-9
      1. Pottery craft. 2. Ceramic tableware. I. Title.
   TT920 .T7524 2001
   738—dc21

                                           00-063488

10 9 8 7 6 5 4 3 2 1

Published by Lark Books, a division of
Sterling Publishing Co., Inc.
387 Park Avenue South, New York, N.Y. 10016

© 2001, Kathy Triplett

Distributed in Canada by Sterling Publishing,
c/o Canadian Manda Group, One Atlantic Ave., Suite 105
Toronto, Ontario, Canada M6K 3E7

Distributed in the U.K. by:
Guild of Master Craftsman Publications Ltd.
Castle Place
166 High Street
Lewes
East Sussex
England
BN7 1XU
Tel: (+ 44) 1273 477374
Fax: (+ 44) 1273 478606
Email: pubs@thegmcgroup.com
Web: www.gmcpublications.com

Distributed in Australia by Capricorn Link (Australia) Pty Ltd., P.O. Box 6651, Baulkham Hills, Business Centre
NSW 2153, Australia

If you have questions or comments about this book, please contact:
Lark Books
50 College St.
Asheville, NC 28801
(828) 253-0467

Printed in China

ISBN 1-57990-204-9

On the cover: **Mary Kay Botkins**, *Luncheon Set,* 4" x 9" x 9" (10.2 x 22.9 x 22.9 cm), 1999. Grolleg porcelain, drape-molded plates, extruded slab for bowl; glazed; Δ6 oxidation. Photo by Neil Pickett

Opposite: **David Crane**, *Platter Group,* 2000. Stoneware, slab made with drape and hump molds; polychrome glaze resist; Δ10. Photo by Jim McLeod

Dedicated to two men in my life who encouraged me to be an adventuresome cook and eater, my husband, Jim, and my father, Walter.

Table of Contents

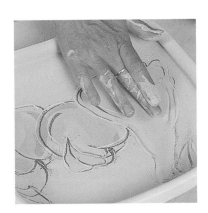

Introduction

MY GRANDFATHER made tiny salt servers out of sea shells and carved little wooden spoons for special dinners when I was young. Fat deviled eggs were nestled on dimpled plates, and corn on the cob rotated in a special ceramic butter boat. These "special use" servers were, and still are, a marvel to me.

Making tableware for yourself and others affords you the opportunity to coordinate special serving dishes with culinary ideas. I was inspired to make the cone-shaped bowl that's part of the set in Chapter 4, for example, by a shrimp and corn recipe, which involved using corn husks shooting up from a bowl on a pedestal. Do you love to serve soups in wide, flat, open bowls that make the soup the centerpiece of the meal? Do you prefer to eat with chopsticks from small bowls with pointed bottoms? Perhaps someone you know wants an entire set of oversized oval tableware, complete with oyster plates. When you're handbuilding, as

you'll see in the pages that follow, you can make bowls, plates, and other pieces to suit nearly any style or need.

We can learn an interesting lesson from the aluminum trays that contain TV dinners or the compartmentalized dishes used to serve meals on airplanes: a plate doesn't have to be round. A handbuilt plate can easily have any silhouette. The point of handbuilding is not to imitate the look of wheel-thrown pottery, but to create pieces that embrace the unique qualities a slab of clay offers. For the beginning potter, shaping clay by hand offers a great advantage over working with a potter's wheel. You don't have to spend that long period of time up front learning to "center" and "throw," so you can achieve success relatively quickly.

The tools you need to begin are few: ordinary items such as a rolling pin, a sponge, and a knife. This book will guide you through choosing your tools and the right clay, making a slab (if you've ever made biscuits, you're way ahead of the game), and glazing and firing. Even if you're already a production potter but you've avoided handbuilding because you imagine it requires a big investment of time, you may find techniques here that could speed your production—and add unique items to your line of wheel work.

The place settings in this book are mere suggestions. A cup from one project could easily be adapted to go with another setting. Each of the plate designs could be altered in terms of shape or size. And any of the pieces could be glazed differently. Though the glazing directions that accompany each project are simple and straightforward, you can see from the photos of other artists' work throughout the book that there are a thousand ways to experiment with surface decoration. Plates and platters in particular—in any shape—delight the potter interested in surface decoration. They offer a broad, smooth surface you can treat like a canvas, ready for your addition of paint or design.

As I contemplated tableware designs for this book, I started noticing how chefs who specialize in various cooking styles present their dishes. I asked several from different traditions to share their opinions on food presentation—you'll find their advice throughout the book.

The ritual of preparing and serving food must be one of the oldest human customs of all, and maybe one of the few remaining meaningful ones. Performing this ritual with handmade pieces makes it all the more rich, as we celebrate the relationship between the objects and the physical act of making them. We could feed ourselves just as easily with a manufactured plate or even a paper one. But a handmade piece, one that reveals the mark of its maker, reminds us of our connection to the physical world around us, to those we eat with, and to the traditions we create together.

CHAPTER 1

Getting Started

CLAY

Moist clay is an irresistible material to be around. From babies to adults, no one can resist poking a finger into it, making an impression, squeezing it into a shape, and feeling how slippery it gets when it's wet. Clay is not the same thing as mud, and working with it is more fun than making mud pies. Plasticity is the property that makes clay so intriguing. Because of it, clay is pliable and holds whatever shape you bend it into. Plasticity is due to the fineness of clay's particles and to their flat shape. Water between these flat particles allows them to both cling together and slide against each other.

Many types of naturally occurring clays exist, all with different types of impurities, from organic matter to small particles of other minerals. These impurities are what give different clays their varying qualities of color and texture. For example, different amounts of iron in a clay make the color range from gray to tan to red-brown to dark brown. Larger particles of metals, such as manganese, may produce a speckled effect in *fired* clay, which is clay that has been baked in the intense heat of a kiln.

The larger particles in clay provide tooth and contribute to a clay's workability and

The Potter's Language

Potters, like people in any professional group, have developed a vocabulary they use when talking about tools, materials, and techniques related to their work. I'll introduce you to lots of terms from that vocabulary throughout this chapter. Those that are italicized, along with many others, are also defined in the Glossary, beginning on page 139.

strength. A sculptural clay for large pieces will generally require more tooth than a clay for wheel throwing or smaller pieces.

A potter may dig up and use clay in its natural state with only minimal processing to remove rocks and debris. Historically, centers of pottery production developed around particularly abundant clay deposits. Today, however, clay deposits are mined commercially, and clay suppliers combine different clays along with other materials to make *clay bodies* that are more suitable for the particular needs of potters. You can purchase dry ingredients to mix your own clay bodies; multitudes of formulas exist. Or, you can alter a formula to invent your own clay body. Clay mixers, called pug mills, combine the dry ingredients with water to make clay. They can also combine recycled clay slurry, a mixture of clay and water, in with the batch so that it will begin to age a little faster, thereby becoming more plastic.

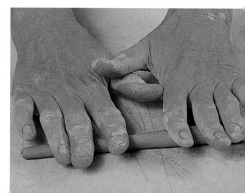

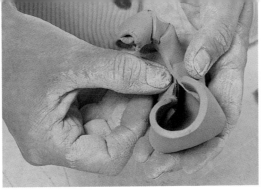

Many potters now select and purchase clays that are formulated and mixed by a supplier to suit their particular needs and aesthetic tastes. The clay typically comes ready to use in 25-pound (11.35 kg) plastic bags. A new bag of commercially prepared clay rarely needs any preparation for handbuilding. If, however, the consistency is uneven, you will need to *wedge* the clay, or knead it to redistribute moisture and eliminate lumps and bubbles. Wedging is best done on a sturdy work surface that is lower than a normal worktable, roughly at arms' length. Put the force of your whole body into leaning on the lump of clay, turning it slightly, and then pressing again until, when the lump is sliced with a wire, it looks and feels consistent. Try not to trap air inside the

Wedging clay

lump by folding it over on itself. Recycled clay may require a lot of wedging.

Clays According to Firing Temperatures

Clays are referred to as *earthenware, stoneware,* or *porcelain,* according to the temperature at which they will harden and become nonporous or *mature* in the kiln, and according to what they're composed of.

At first, the choices of clay types are baffling. But once you begin to consider your preferences in terms of color, texture, workability, shrinkage, and porosity, you can easily narrow your choices.

Each clay body has its own *maturation point* during firing—a point at which it vitrifies, becoming dense, waterproof, glasslike, and impervious to acids. It is not a precise temperature but a range, usually stated in terms of *cones*. Cones represent a system of measurement of firing temperatures in ceramics. (For example, a mid-range porcelain may be

Bryan Hiveley, *Instinct,* 13" (33 cm) in diameter; 2000. Earthenware, slab, pinched rim; sgraffito, underglazes, glazed; Δ03. Photo by artist

Molly Lithgo, *Dressing Pitcher*, 6" × 9" × 4" (15.2 × 22.9 × 10.2 cm), 2000. Earthenware, pinch pot with coil and slab additions; multiple underglazes with clear glaze; Δ3 oxidation. Photo by Jim Rientjes

rated from Δ5 to Δ7.) They are small, pyramid-shaped pieces of clay formulated to bend and melt when the kiln has reached a certain temperature. Potters place the cones so that they can be viewed (wearing protective glasses) by peering through the kiln's peepholes. Ranges of temperature are designated by numbers, with, for example, Δ022 being very low, Δ05 being higher and representing a typical *bisque-firing* temperature (the first firing of unglazed ware to remove all moisture and make it easier to handle), Δ6 being a mid-range temperature, and Δ10 being higher yet, for a stoneware or porcelain range.

See Appendix A for a listing of cone numbers with the corresponding temperatures. (When you use the list, be sure to note that cone numbers such as Δ03 and Δ3, for example, are not the same; Δ03 is lower than Δ3.) Why not just use a thermometer (or pyrometer as it is called at these temperatures)? The reason is that cones are a more accurate measure of both temperature *and* time, so

they better represent how your clay and glazes may be melting in the kiln. For example, a glaze may melt at a slightly lower temperature if it has been exposed to a longer heat cycle.

Earthenware clays are *low-fire clays*, ones that mature below 2000°F (1093°C). They may be white or brown, with the brown versions sometimes referred to as "terra-cotta," meaning fired earth. Though earthenware will never be quite as strong, dense, or as vitrified as stoneware, it can, if fired to maturity, be strong, chip resistant, microwave and oven safe, and make long-lasting pots, without being either dense or vitrified. Even a very mature earthenware body may still have a 10-percent absorption rate. However, if the nature of the clay's pore structure permits it to absorb water without expanding, the absorption rate won't necessarily cause glaze to craze or crack into fine lines. An earthenware body will also be stronger if it does not contain grog (ground-fired clay) or sand, in spite of the fact that these additions may

C. Edgar Gilliam Jr., *Rooster Plate*, 13½" (34.3 cm) in diameter, 1999. Stoneware, slab over hump mold; incised with needle tool, bisque fired, washed with red iron oxide and frit; Δ6. Photo by Michael Noa

improve its workability. Earthenware should be fired to maturity and glazed with a smooth, craze- and blemish-free glaze to achieve its maximum strength. Though there are few drawbacks to the porous nature of earthenware, one is that absorbed water will heat up if you place an earthenware pot in a microwave, causing its handles to become hot. A second is that in hot, moist climates, mold can grow under the glaze near an unglazed foot. Coating the foot with a *terra sigillata*, a slip made of the fine particles of clay, will help to seal it. One advantage to the porosity is that it gives the body an insulation quality; coffee stays hot longer in an earthenware mug.

Stoneware and **porcelain** are *high-fire clays* that vitrify at temperatures higher than 2000°F (1093°C). Stoneware may be creamy white, gray, tan, or brown, but porcelain is very white, usually fine-toothed, waterproof without glaze, and may be translucent when thin. Because of these qualities, porcelain is especially popular for tableware. Its smooth white surface causes glaze colors to be especially brilliant. Manufacturers can add ceramic stains or oxides to white clays, such as porcelain, or you can add them yourself to create a broad palette of colored clays.

A wide variety of clay bodies that fire at mid-range is also now available to suit the needs of potters whose kilns are rated to fire at a maximum temperature of Δ6. Even potters with high-temperature gas kilns have found working with clays that fire in this middle range to be a good energy-saving alternative. Both porcelain and stoneware bodies have been formulated to mature at this range.

What happens if you fire the clay at the wrong temperature? If you fire it higher than its recommended range, your clay may bubble, warp, or even melt. If you fire it lower than the maturation temperature, the clay may remain porous and able to absorb water, which in turn may cause the glaze to flake off. It can also chip or break easily, and when tapped, it may yield a thud instead of a clear, high-pitched ring. In other words, firing to the proper vitrification point is important when making tableware.

Shrinkage

All clay shrinks as it dries, usually about five percent. Then it shrinks another five percent or so when it is fired to maturity. Some supplier catalogs provide the shrinkage at different cone temperatures for various clays, with the highest percent of shrinkage listed corresponding with the highest temperature. Shrinkage causes big surprises for beginners; large platters can come out of the kiln looking like saucers!

Learning how to calculate shrinkage yourself will help you avoid such disappointing surprises. One easy way is to make a clay ruler like the one shown here. I like to make one for each new clay I use, writing the shrinkage percentages on the strip.

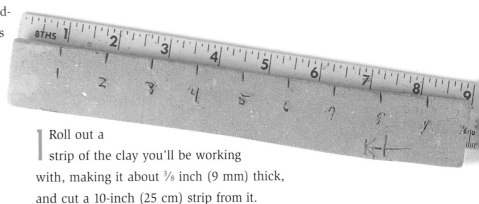

1 Roll out a strip of the clay you'll be working with, making it about ⅜ inch (9 mm) thick, and cut a 10-inch (25 cm) strip from it.

Margaret F. Patterson, *Tea Service*, teapot 8" × 10" × 5" (20.3 × 25.4 × 12.7 cm), creamer 3" × 3" × 2" (7.6 × 7.6 × 5.1 cm), sugar 3" × 5" × 2" (7.6 × 12.7 × 5.1 cm), 1998. Earthenware, slabs; embossed using roulette; Δ03 oxidation. Photo by artist

2 Either press a ruler with raised numbers into it to make an impression, or use the ruler as a guide to mark off accurate dimensions in the clay strip.

3 Allow the strip to dry, then place it beside the ruler and measure how much it has shrunk. Next, fire it to the bisque temperature, measure the change, then fire it again to the maturation point, and again measure the change.

Keep a record of these measurements. They'll come in handy for many things, such as calculating shrinkage if you need to make a new lid for a piece that has already dried or been fired. To precisely reproduce a certain size, first use the shrunken clay ruler to determine the measurement you want to end up with. Then, use a real ruler to measure out your raw clay piece. In the drying and firing process, the piece will shrink so that it matches the measurement on the shrunken clay ruler.

Cracking and Warping

Shrinkage leads to the most ubiquitous of potters' dilemmas: cracking and warping. Both are caused by a buildup of stress in the clay, which is often related to uneven shrinkage caused by uneven drying. In general, you should cover pieces with plastic to slow the drying and to make it more uniform. Thick parts of a piece will dry more slowly than thin parts. So, when you wrap a piece in plastic to dry it, you may want to wrap the handle, for example, more tightly, so it doesn't dry out completely before the body of the pitcher dries. In addition, edges dry more rapidly than the bottoms of vessels, so drying pieces upside down also helps even out the drying process. Don't dry your pieces in drafty areas; drafts may cause one side of a piece to dry more quickly than another. And don't leave a pool of water or slip in the bottom of a cup or bowl that you set aside to dry.

Betsy Rosenmiller, *Tray with Four Cups*, 4¼" × 17" × 4" (10.8 × 43.2 × 10.2 cm), 1999. Porcelain, press molded then formed; glazed; fired to Δ5 with glaze, refired to Δ019. Photo by artist

Bending a clay slab after it has stiffened too much can also cause cracking, as can joining pieces of clay of differing moisture contents. I often make all the parts for a piece, then wrap them all up together in plastic and let them sit overnight before I assemble them. This allows the moisture to equalize. The most critical period in shrinkage is when clay goes from its wet to its *leather-hard* stage, the point at which it has dried somewhat but can still be carved or joined. The leather-hard stage is when almost half of the shrinkage may occur, so it's when your pieces are most vulnerable.

Tip

To create the perfect plastic cover for your drying pieces if you live in a humid climate, fold a plastic sheet and use a hole punch to perforate it to allow some air to enter through it.

Warping is a problem even for commercial tableware manufacturers. Sometimes, their solution is to fire to a vitrification temperature first, with the ware stacked in the kiln in a way that restricts warping, and then to conduct the *glaze firing* (the firing that melts the glaze) at a lower temperature. Most studio potters who try this method find it difficult to glaze such nonporous ware, so they've come up with other ways to reduce warpage. One is to use a slightly less plastic clay. (The more plastic a clay body is, the more it shrinks, and the more it shrinks, the more stresses are built up in it.) Another is, when working with slab rollers (see page 21), to roll out each slab from several different directions, rather than simply passing each through the rollers once. A third is to slow the drying process to make the drying more even.

When making tableware, you should dry plates on a flat surface, and you shouldn't pick them up by the edge before they are past the leather-hard stage. The stress produced in moving a freshly made slab of clay can cause distortion that may not show up until the final firing. If your plates sag or slump in the glaze firing, the design of the plate itself could be at fault. The plates may need more support in some strategic location, or you may need to make them thicker. You might want to reposition the feet or add a temporary small wad of clay on an unglazed part of the bottom for additional support through the firing.

Sometimes, the only solution for clay that continually cracks or warps is to try a different clay.

Tips

■ If I think the bottom of a plate is too close to the kiln shelf and could sag a bit during the glaze firing, I stick a small disc of clay on a little waxed circle in the middle of the bottom of a plate (where I have signed the piece) before the firing. I remove the disk after the firing.

■ Handles that are too heavy can cause cups meant to be round to become misshapen. To remedy the problem, dry and fire the cups on an angle. You can either prop up each cup so the weight of the handle isn't pulling on the cup, or you can angle the ware board that they sit on for drying and the kiln shelf that they sit on during firing.

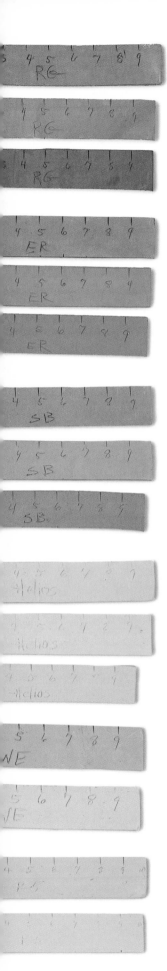

Color

The color of raw clay does not precisely represent the color it will be when it's fired. A brown clay may fire to a pinkish color at the bisque temperature and then be red-brown to dark brown at maturity. A gray clay may end up cream or white. Speckles of granular manganese, not evident in the unfired clay, may be quite obvious in the finished product, even showing through an opaque glaze. The photos on the left provide some examples of how the colors of different clays change through a firing process. The clay color can also completely change the look and surface quality of a glaze. A white clay will make the glaze over it appear much brighter than it would be on a brown clay. A darker clay may give a glaze more variation and texture. You'll also alter the color of your clay if you use a colored *slip*, a coating of clay, water, and other ingredients, to make the slip fit the clay body or to change the background color of the glaze in certain areas of the piece you're making.

Porosity

Different clays also vary in their degree of porosity at maturity. In the clay section of a supplier's catalogue, you'll often find a listing of absorption rates at several different cone temperatures for each clay body. The higher the cone temperature, the less absorption there will be, which means the clay will be less porous. You can also measure porosity yourself. Fire a piece of unglazed clay to its maturing temperature and then weigh it on a gram scale. Then, soak the clay piece in water for about eight hours, wipe it off, and weigh it again. The percentage gain in weight indicates the clay's porosity. It may range from 10 percent to less than 1 percent. When choosing clay for making tableware, look for a low-porosity percentage. A good-fitting glaze (see page 39 for a description of glaze fit) can help to make a porous clay more suitable for tableware. With majolica ware, made of a red earthenware body, it's often a good idea to apply a terra-sigillata slip to the unglazed portions to further seal them and make them less porous. You apply terra-sigillata at the greenware stage, before the ware has been fired.

Buying Clay

If you're buying ready-mixed clay, consider buying in bulk to save money. Often, different kinds of clay can be combined for a quantity price break. Clay can be stored indefinitely; in fact, it improves with age, since it becomes more plastic. Freezing

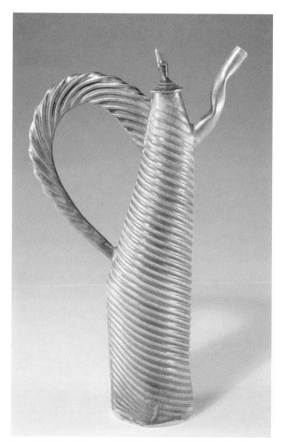

Laurie Rolland, *Teapot*, 7" (18 cm) tall, 1999. Handbuilt stoneware; washes of oxide and glaze; Δ6. Photo by artist

doesn't ruin it, but clay that's been frozen does require reworking to redistribute the water evenly. Clay will dry out even in plastic bags over a period of time, but double bagging can help keep it moist longer. You can also add some water (just a light sprinkling or spraying) to the bags from time to time.

Recycling Clay

Clay work seldom looks better than it does at the leather-hard stage (when your piece is assembled and somewhat dry). If you don't like what you see then, toss it on the scrap pile. Glaze can't rescue an unconvincing piece. And remember, your next piece will almost always be better. All clay, before it is fired, can be recycled and reused. Recycling is easiest if you wait until the clay is completely dry (when it slakes down quickly in water to form a slurry). Spread the slurry on a ware board or a plaster slab to dry, then wedge it or knead it, and bag it. This process is not much fun, so some potters toss out their scraps to save time. But I don't worry about the added work time. I figure, just like bottle recycling, it's good to do a small part in preserving natural resources. Some pottery schools are eager to get rid of accumulated buckets of scraps. Volunteer to recycle it to obtain some free clay, and you'll also find that you are rewarded with enough lost pottery tools (accidentally tossed in with the scraps) to last a lifetime! Of course, clay you get this way could be a mixture of several

Isabella St. John, *Cod Table Setting*, dinner plate 12" (30.5 cm), side plate 8" (20.3 cm), bowl 6" × 2½" (15.2 × 6.4 cm), mug 4" × 3" (10.2 × 7.6 cm), napkin ring 2½" × 2" (6.4 × 5.1 cm), 1997. Slab, textured, thrown, torn, and pieced back together; impressed surface; Δ6 oxidation. Photo by Ned Pratt

different kinds, so you'll need to test it to determine firing temperature and final color.

To keep from having too many buckets of scrap clay sitting around the studio, toss your scraps into a plastic bag as you work, spray them with water, and allow the bag to sit for awhile so the moisture evens out. Then, wedge the clay or roll out slabs, folding and rerolling the slabs several times to make the clay more consistent and to check for air bubbles.

You may find one way to cut down on the amount you have to recycle is to cut the shapes you need out of a freshly rolled slab instead of waiting until the slab is leather hard. Either approach to cutting out your shapes is workable (as I'll explain in the Techniques section later), but scrap pieces cut from a freshly rolled slab can be reused right away; you don't have to put them through the recycling process.

TOOLS, EQUIPMENT, AND SUPPLIES

You may be overwhelmed by all the new ceramic equipment on the market today. You really don't have to have a studio equipped with every different tool to get started. Remember that many beautiful works from the past were created with little more than two hands and some fuel—and many are created the same way today. No amount of tools can compensate for experience with the clay, so go ahead and get some basic tools and get your hands dirty first, then decide what to add in terms of additional tools and equipment later.

Basic Tools

You can probably find a few basic items in your kitchen to get started, including a wooden rolling pin (for rolling out clay slabs by hand), a knife, a sponge, and a fork for scoring the clay. Scrounge around for some scraps of plywood or sheetrock (referred to as ware boards in the pottery studio) on which to roll slabs, a wire to cut off lumps of clay from the blocks they come in, a needle tool for cutting soft slabs and for numerous other jobs, a few small stiff brushes for applying slip, a spray water bottle to mist clay as you work to keep it from drying too fast, a 1- x 2-inch (2.5 x 5 cm) wooden stick or a paddle, and some buckets, and you'll be able to make just about anything.

Additional Tools

Next, you can refine your studio with the following tools:

METAL RULER. This will serve as a straightedge. I like metal because your knife won't cut it, and it won't warp when it's exposed to moisture.

SCORING TOOLS. Made of stiff wires extending from a handle. They come with either thick crinkly wires or thin straight wires. The type you need depends on the scale of your work. (Thick wires are better for large-scale work, and thinner ones are better for small-scale work.)

LOOP TRIMMING TOOLS. For carving designs into stiff clay.

METAL OR RUBBER RIB. To smooth seams. A metal rib with a serrated edge also works well for scoring or texturizing clay.

METAL HOLE CUTTERS. They come in varying diameters.

A 90° ANGLE OR T-SQUARE

WOODEN DOWELS. Get them in different sizes, from ¼ inch (6 mm) to as thick as they come.

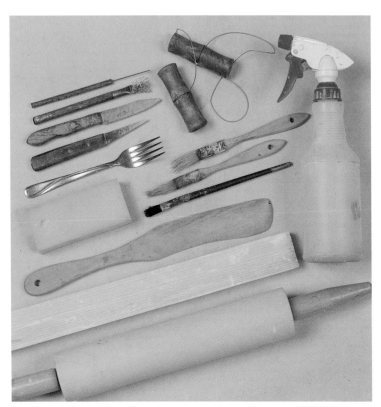

Beginning top left: needle tool, wire scoring tool, knives, fork, sponge, brushes, wooden paddles, rolling pin, cut-off wire, spray bottle

A PONY ROLLER. A tool with two wooden dowels, one rounded and one straight, useful for smoothing edges.

KNIVES. Different sizes and types, such as a long-bladed fettling knife; a sharp, pointed, thin-bladed knife; and a simple kitchen knife with a rounded blade.

A TURNTABLE. Either a metal one or a lazy-Susan type.

CARDBOARD, PAPER, AND SCISSORS. For design and template work.

Tools such as a **SABER SAW, SANDPAPER,** and a **WOOD RASP.** Handy for making molds.

A STURDY WORKTABLE. Make it one on which you can pound.

SHEETS OF CANVAS. Use them to cover your work surface and ware boards.

SHEETS OF LIGHTWEIGHT PLASTIC. Prevent clay from drying too fast.

MOP AND SPONGES. Wet cleaning is critical in the clay studio. Never use a broom or duster; inhaling clay dust can be hazardous.

SAFETY TOOLS AND EQUIPMENT. You'll want a respirator rated for dust, welder's goggles for looking into a kiln during a firing, and heat-resistant gloves for removing a kiln's peephole plugs during a firing and for removing still-warm pieces from a kiln after a firing.

You'll also find that tools made for other purposes can be useful in the clay studio. From dental tools to frog gigging implements to cookie cutters, all sorts of found objects can be useful texturizing and cutting tools. Some of the most enjoyable tools to use are the ones you make yourself or the ones someone else has made. My favorite brush, for example, is made of my dog Zipper's tail hair.

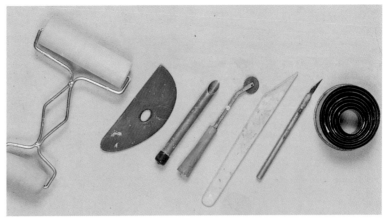

From left: pony roller, rubber rib, hole cutter, serrated roller, modeling tool, craft knife, cookie cutters

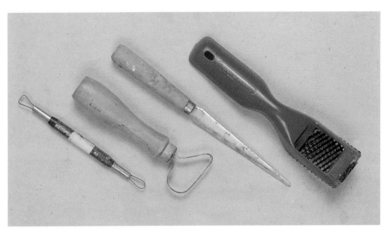

From left: loop trimming tools, fettling knife, wood rasp

Turntable

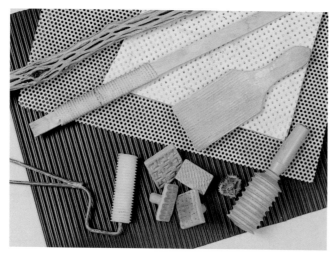

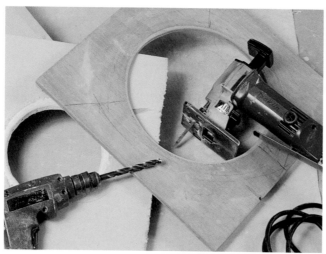

Clockwise from top left: a variety of texturizing tools, tools for mixing glazes, tools for spraying glazes, a drill and saber saw, used for making molds from plywood and drywall board

Glazing Tools

If you decide to mix your own glazes, you'll need a few tools, such as a gram scale for measuring glaze ingredients and a large and small sieve or screen, with a mesh size of 60 or 80. You'll also need containers, spatulas, scoops, a dust respirator, brushes, and sponges. Additional items that are nice to have (but not required) include glaze tongs, a squeeze bottle for glaze trailing, and a high-speed drill with a mixer attachment.

If you want to spray your glazes on, you'll need a spray gun and an air compressor. This operation should be performed in a booth,

Spraying in a spray booth

complete with an air exhaust fan. You can either purchase a spray booth or build one yourself. You can also spray outdoors, but the weather can make it tricky. Always wear a respirator when spraying. An airbrush is handy for applying oxides or underglazes, but to glaze a whole pot by spraying, you'll need a spray gun with a quart-size (.95 L) container.

Slicing clay

Major Equipment
SLAB ROLLER

A professional studio where handbuilding is part of the production will likely feature a slab roller. The rollers are usually manually operated, though an electric option does exist. A slab roller can make even and consistent slabs quickly by passing the clay between or under rollers to compress it into a uniform thickness. The size of the roller will determine how easily a piece of clay can be rolled into a slab and how thick a piece you can start with. You can adjust the thickness of the slab you produce by raising or lowering the roller. Some rollers have Masonite panels that are added or removed to change the thickness. If you work alone, you may find a large slab roller unnecessary, since larger, heavier slabs often require two people to move them. Remember, too, that the size of what you produce is limited by your kiln size.

Making a Slab with a Slab Roller

1 Slice off several blocks of clay about an inch (2.5 cm) thick, and position them together on a heavy piece of canvas.

2 Pound them together and place another piece of canvas on top. Adjust the thickness and position the sandwich in front of the rollers.

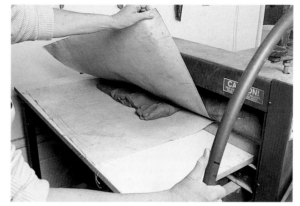

Sending the sandwich through the rollers

3 Send the sandwich through the rollers. If this requires a great deal of effort, several passes through may be necessary to reduce the thickness gradually, especially if the clay is somewhat stiff. A heavy canvas, such as 12-ounce (336 g) duck, which resists wrinkling, is necessary. (You can also use just one large piece of canvas. Place the clay on top of it, then fold the canvas over the clay, sending the folded edge through or under the rollers first.)

4 Peel off (or fold back) the top canvas and use the bottom canvas to transport the slab to ware boards or your work surface. Try not to distort the slab too much in moving it, as this distortion could cause warping later.

Tip

To lift a slab without distorting it, place a ware board on top of the slab and flip the whole sandwich over, then lift it.

A

Rebecca Koop, *Cups and Saucers*,
saucer 6" (15.2 cm) across, cup 4"
(10.2 cm) tall, 1995. Earthenware,
slab, extruded handles; majolica glaze,
stains, oxides; Δ04.
Photo by Janet Ryan

B

Mary Kay Botkins, *Casserole*, 5½" ×
10" × 5" (14 × 25.4 × 12.7 cm), 1999.
Grolleg porcelain, extruded slab,
slumped lid, folded handle; glazed; Δ6
oxidation. Photo by Neil Pickett

C

Robert Pillers, *Fish Platter*, 3¾" × 20"
× 11½" (9.5 × 50.8 × 29.2 cm), 1999.
Stoneware, slab over plaster slump
mold, extruded feet and handles;
glazed, stamped decorations; Δ11
reduction. Photo by Jerry Anthony

D

John Hesselberth, *Pitcher*, 11" × 9" ×
4" (27.9 × 22.9 × 10.2 cm), 1998.
Stoneware, soft slab, pulled handle;
textured, multiple slips and glazes; Δ6
oxidation. Photo by artist

A

B

D

C
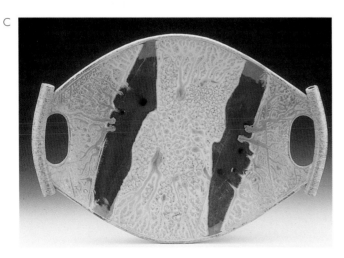

EXTRUDER

The extruder can produce seamless tubes of clay, either hollow or solid, or any number of different shapes in any length you want. Like slab rollers, extruders are also usually hand operated, but you can find extruders with electric motors. Some models come with a large enough opening to produce a piece as wide as 14 inches (35 cm). You can purchase dies in simple shapes, or you can make your own by using marine-grade plywood. You can also find metal laser-cutting businesses that can quickly make precision cuts in metal

Extruder dies

plates to your specifications. If you make your own dies from marine plywood, try beveling the edges to make the extrusions flow more smoothly through the dies. Also, seal the plywood with a wood sealer.

The extruder takes some effort to clean between uses. Some potters who use different types of clay in the same extruder save cleaning time by putting the clay inside a plastic bag with a hole in the end before loading it into the extruder barrel.

THE KILN

Your most important equipment need is a kiln (unfortunately, the kitchen oven just doesn't get hot enough!). Taking a class can be a great way to get access to a kiln while you ponder the different types available and consider whether you want to buy or build one.

Early kilns were simply pits in the ground, fueled with wood or dung. The temperatures reached were low and the ware remained porous. By today's standards, it would be unhygienic for use with food. Today, potters typically use electric kilns or those fueled by gas or wood.

Electric kilns are manufactured in many sizes, shapes, and temperature ranges, are

Using an extruder

John Britt, *Pin Stripe Tea*, 12" × 5" × 4" (30.5 × 12.7 × 10.2 cm), 1998. Slab-built porcelain, extruded spout; waxed white lines and painted-on glaze; Δ10 reduction in gas alpine kiln. Photo by artist

easy to use, and offer predictable results. Computer-controlled kilns can even be programmed to practically fire themselves. For safety's sake, however, I always watch closely at the end of the firing to make sure everything has shut off according to plan. Electric firings are suitable only for *oxidation firings*, or firings with an ample oxygen supply. *Reduction firings*, in which oxygen in the kiln is deliberately reduced to cause clay

and/or glaze to change color, will take extra toll on the elements of an electric kiln.

Gas or wood-burning kilns are more likely than electric kilns to be constructed by hand, although one can buy gas kilns. Gas kilns may have burners designed for either natural or bottled gas. One advantage of fuel-burning kilns is that they make reduction firing possible. They're built of firebrick, a brick capable of retaining high temperatures, and sometimes a spun alumina fiber insulating blanket that reduces fuel costs. They can be as large as boats, built into a hillside, or composed of one or more arched brick chambers and a chimney. With a fuel-burning kiln, a potter has a more intimate relationship with the fire, with the adjustment of air-to-fuel ratios, or (with wood fuel) with the amount of ash deposited on the shoulders of pots. The unpredictable aspect of the process adds excitement, and the fire seems to play its own role in where surfaces will be flashed and the color changed in both the clay and the glaze. A fuel-burning kiln is also necessary for salt or soda firings.

Kilns get very hot on the outside, so keep combustibles, including your clothing and hair, from coming into contact with the hot exterior. I once leaned a small propane torch against the base of my first kiln, a gas-fired catenary arch kiln. When the small propane cylinder exploded, I burst through the plastic kiln enclosure and ran a quarter mile away before I realized I had to return to see what had happened. Use goggles designed for the bright light of the heat to protect your eyes when you peer through your kiln's peepholes, and wear heat-resistant gloves to remove peephole plugs.

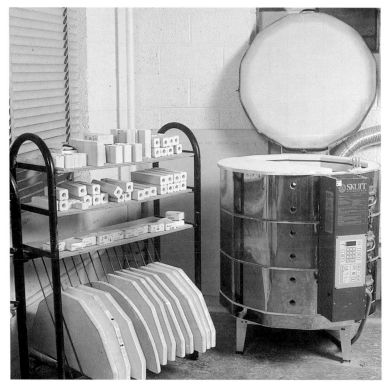

An electric kiln

KILN ACCESSORIES
Temperature Monitors

An experienced potter may be able to gauge the temperature in the kiln merely from the color, which ranges from dull red at 1000°F (538°C) to bright yellow at 2000°F (1093°C). If you'd rather have some help, you've got several options.

Digital Monitors and Pyrometers

Electric kilns may have a digital programmer that displays the temperature at all times. You can also use a pyrometer to monitor the rise and fall of temperatures in the kiln. A pyrometer has one or more probes, each of which measures the temperature in a different part of the kiln. Pyrometers are also available as handheld digital models, so that only one is necessary to monitor several kilns. Be careful not to damage the tip that is inserted into the kiln when loading ware for a firing; it becomes brittle and fragile with use. Temperature monitoring is also essential for firing crystalline glazes, which require a

cooling cycle that is extended at critical stages to make the crystals grow.

Cones

As discussed earlier, pyrometric cones are also used to gauge rising temperatures in the kiln. Manufactured to melt and bend at specific temperatures and over specific lengths of time, cones come in two sizes. Use the smaller size in the *kiln sitter*, the automatic turn-off system in many electric kilns, and the larger size in cone packs, small wads of moist clay or specially made cone holders, each with a row of three cones protruding at a slight angle.

A cone pack

In the center of your cone pack, place what is called the witness cone, the one that will melt when the kiln reaches the peak temperature you want. Just in front of it, place the warning cone, which melts at one temperature notch lower. On the other side, place the cone that melts at one notch higher, to indicate the possibility of overfiring. (In a reduction firing, you'll use an additional cone to indicate when the early stages of reduction need to begin. In a bisque firing, where tempera-

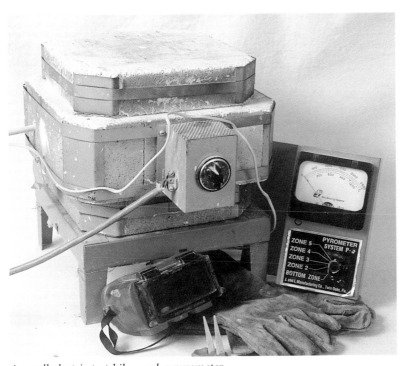

A small electric test kiln, and a pyrometer

WORK SPACE AND WORKING SAFE

Unless you anticipate producing lots of pieces all at once, you don't need much work space to get started. (My first studio was a closet with shelves arranged up to the ceiling!)

It's safest to keep your clay-working area away from your kitchen and living space, because breathing clay or glaze dust is harmful to your health. Always wet clean with a mop or sponge rather than use a broom or vacuum, unless you're using a vacuum made specifically for clay dust. Perform as many operations as you can on the clay before it dries, not afterwards. Wear a dust respirator and plastic gloves when mixing glazes or if you have to work on dry clay. Be sure the kiln area is well ventilated, with an attached local exhaust system and/or a whole room exhaust system. Keep any toxic substances labeled and carefully stored. Change clothes after a day in the studio, and wash your clay-working clothes frequently.

ture is not as critical, one cone is usually sufficient.)

Position several cone packs so you can see them through the peepholes in the kiln. Occasionally, if you think there are cool or hot spots in your kiln, you may also want to position a cone somewhere not visible through a peephole, to test temperatures. Every kiln is a little different, and it takes a while to get accustomed to the idiosyncrasies of each one. Make the cone packs in advance, so the clay the cones sit in is com-

pletely dry when you place the packs in the kiln. They can't be used for temperature measurement twice, so discard them after the firing. Cones are important to use even if a pyrometer is available. Pyrometers can fail to function, and cones more accurately indicate glaze melts since they measure both temperature *and* time.

Timers

Electric kilns are often equipped with timers that will turn the kiln off after a set number of hours. Be sure to remember to reset it if you're firing for a longer period of time than your setting allows. With any type of kiln, don't leave town until you're sure it has turned off!

Kiln Furniture

Kiln furniture includes special shelves and different heights of stilts aligned vertically between the shelves, all to allow the kiln to be loaded in the most efficient way possible. Shelves have a maximum temperature at which they can be fired before they begin to sag. They should also be protected from glaze runs with a coat of kiln wash, a mixture of alumina hydrate, kaolin, bentonite,

A kiln loaded with pieces that have just been bisque fired

A

B

A

Pamela Segers, *Illusion*, 2½" × 21" × 21" (6.4 × 53.3 × 53.3 cm), 1999.
Slab-built low-fire white clay; airbrushed velvet underglaze; Δ4.
Photo by Studio III

B

John Berry, *4*, 13¾" × 16⅞" (35 × 43 cm), 1999. Handbuilt and
modeled stoneware body; colored glazes and lusters; Δ9 oxidation.
Photo by Peter White

C

Mia Tyson, *Quiet Restlessness*, 13" × 9½" × 2½" (33 × 24.1 × 6.4 cm),
1999. Slab-built porcelain with pulled handle; sgraffito (black slip
only); Δ10 to Δ11 reduction. Photo by Diane Davis

C

Bonnie Seeman, *Ewer & Tray*, 14" x 11" x 8" (35.6 x 27.9 x 20.3 cm), 1999. Tray: porcelain, slab; textured with a pencil; Δ10. Ewer: porcelain, thrown and shaped, slabs added; textured with a pencil; Δ10. Photo by artist

drips smooth with a Carborundum grinder wheel attached to a drill or a Carborundum hand grinder stone.

TECHNIQUES
Working with Slabs

You can make slabs by hand in several easy ways. One is to slice off a thick piece of clay, hold it with both hands on one edge, and slap it down on a table to stretch it. Repeat this action, holding the slab from a different edge, until it has thinned enough. Another option, one that gives you a nice, even slab, is to use a rolling pin, preferably a big one. Keep turning the slab over as you roll, and use a porous work surface, such as a piece of canvas or sheetrock, to keep the slab from sticking. On either side of the clay you can lay small, flat sticks the thickness of the slab you want. They'll serve as guides for the rolling pin and help you achieve a uniform thickness. (For information about rolling out a slab with a slab roller, see page 21.)

and water mixed to the consistency of cream (see the formula in Appendix B). You paint or spray the wash on the surface of the shelves (covering only the top side, avoiding the bottom and the edges, so that no kiln wash will flake off onto the pots below), and coat the ends of the kiln stilts, as well. If your kiln shelves begin to warp, slip on some safety glasses and use a grinder to remove the wash from one side before turning them over, so they can bend the other way. You could also turn them over only during bisque firings, since the kiln-wash flakes won't hurt the bisqueware. If glaze does adhere to places on the shelves, put on your respirator and safety glasses and grind the

Your clay shapes will have crisper, neater edges if you cut them out of a slab you've allowed to stiffen rather than out of a soft one. However, if you want to end up with fewer clay scraps that have to be recycled before you can reuse them, you may opt for cutting your shapes out of soft clay. If you need to bend or shape your slabs, do so when they're soft, trying not to mar or distort the surface too much, then let them stiffen in the curved shapes before you handle them more.

The trickiest part of handbuilding is getting the clay to just the right softness or hardness to be workable. Nothing is more frustrating than finally getting the time you want in the studio and finding that the slab you made for a big pitcher simply folds up on the table

Sandi Pierantozzi, *Royal Cream & Sugar Set*, 5" × 10" × 6" (12.7 × 25.4 × 15.2 cm), 1998. Slab-built earthenware, brushed-on glazes; Δ04 bisque, Δ05 glaze. Photo by artist

Karl Kuhns and Debra Parker-Kuhns, *Triangle Plate*, 2" × 10" × 10" (5.1 × 25.4 × 25.4 cm), 1998. Porcelain, slab, drape mold; colored slips brushed under clear glaze; Δ8 oxidation. Photo by artists

instead of standing upright. You haul the slab out into the sun so it will stiffen, and before you know it, cracks appear when you try to bend it.

For stiff-slab work, make more slabs than you anticipate needing, and allow them to dry overnight, lightly covered. Of course, this depends on the humidity in your area. If the drying needs to be rushed, try placing the slabs outside in the sun, covering the edges with plastic first. Be patient, and keep several projects going at one time. Hair dryers and even microwaves can sometimes help speed the drying process.

Joining Clay Slabs

The other reason drying is important is that two pieces of clay need to be the same stiffness when they are joined. If they aren't, one piece may already have shrunk more than the other, and the join will be weak or prone to crack. This is one reason why joining different kinds of clay together may be tricky.

You can join soft pieces of clay by firmly pressing and smoothing them together. Join leather-hard pieces by scoring or roughening the surfaces to be joined with a scoring tool, applying slip to each surface with a brush, and then pressing the areas together. The slip you use for joining is simply a clay slurry—a mixture of clay and water. (Some potters like to add a small amount of sodium silicate to the slurry to make the join stronger. They refer to such a mixture as "magic water"; see

Applying slip

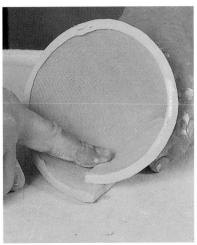

Pressing surfaces together

Paddling a join *Adding a coil*

Bisque Firing

The purpose of a bisque firing is to harden the ware enough to handle it without breaking it. Also, in some cases it is essential that your glaze be applied to bisqueware rather than greenware (a bone-dry clay that has not yet been fired), but not always. The glaze formula for the Spicy Harvest Setting (page 50), for example, worked for me when I tried it on the greenware plates. Typically, glaze formulas that include a high percentage of clay are the ones that work best on pieces

Appendix C for a formula.) Sometimes, it may seem you can stick a couple of pieces of clay together without all the bother of scoring and applying slip, but once the clay is dry, the pieces can easily fall apart if they haven't been joined properly. To smooth and strengthen the join, paddle it with a wooden tool. You can also add a small coil to strengthen a join and round its angles.

To prevent cracking and warping, it's always best to dry the pieces slowly. Large, heavy plates or platters need to be able to contract freely as they dry and may need to be dried upside down. At least a week is necessary for medium-sized pieces to dry. Larger, thicker work requires even more time to dry thoroughly.

Brushing dust off a bisque-fired platter

that will be fired only once. When glazing greenware, however, there's always the danger that thin clay parts may absorb water from the glaze so much that they simply dissolve in the glaze bucket; so for beginners, it's a good idea to bisque fire everything first. It's also very difficult, if not impossible, to rinse off a bad glaze application if your piece hasn't been bisque fired.

Since it's okay for pieces in a bisque firing to touch each other, they can be stacked, as long as they are free to contract without being inhibited by another piece inside. Rim to rim or foot to foot is a good rule of thumb, and never pile too much weight on thinner pieces. Kiln manufacturers recommend that ware be at least 1 inch

Tip

When you're determining the size of plates or other pieces of tableware you plan to handbuild, check first to see what your dishwasher will accommodate.

A

B

C

D

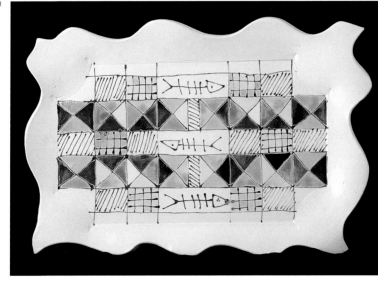

A
Rosie Souter Paschall, *Summer*, 16" × 17" × 2" (40.6 × 43.2 × 5.1 cm), 1999. Earthenware, hand-rolled slab; carved, glazed, stained; Δ06. Photo by Pro Photo

B
Kathy Steinsberger, *Flamingo Road*, 10" × 12" × 5" (25.4 × 30.5 × 12.7 cm), 1998. Earthenware, slab and coil; underglazes and clear glaze; Δ04 and Δ05. Photo by Doug Van Zandt

C
Jenny Lou Sherburne, *Etruscan Pitcher*, 18" × 14" × 14" (45.7 × 35.6 × 35.6 cm), 1996. Stoneware, coil built with leaf form additions; carving, engobes, glazes; Δ06 and Δ04. Photo by Steve Meltzer

D
Angela Gallia, *Untitled*, 8" × 13" (20.3 × 33 cm), 1999. Slab-built earthenware; stain, wax resist, glaze; Δ02 bisque, Δ04 glaze. Photo by Lonie Leigh Lawrence

A
Sandi Pierantozzi, *Soup Tureen*, 11" × 12" × 11"
(27.9 × 30.5 × 27.9 cm), 1999. Slab-built earthenware; carved, brushed-on glazes; Δ04 bisque,
Δ05 glaze. Photo by artist

B
Mouse Scharfenaker, *Pear Platter*, 19½" × 4" × 1"
(49.5 × 10.2 × 2.5 cm), 1999. Earthenware,
hand-pulled slab, formed on mold; majolica and
colored overglazes; Δ06 oxidation.
Photo by John Bonath

C
Betsy Rosenmiller, *Serving Dish*, 2" × 8½" × 6"
(5.1 × 21.6 × 15.2 cm), 1999. Porcelain, handbuilt, textured; china paint, glaze; Δ018 china
paint, Δ5 glaze. Photo by artist

A

B

C

Betsy Rosenmiller, *Cruet Set*, 6" × 5" × 4" (15.2 × 12.7 × 10.2 cm), 1998. Porcelain, slab, pressed; Δ018 china paint, Δ5 glaze. Photo by artist

(2.5 cm) away from the wall of the kiln, but I break this rule all the time. Usually, I try to make sure large plates are away from the wall and not on the bottom shelf. This protects them from uneven heat, which could cause cracking.

When picking up greenware to put it in the kiln, cradle the pieces carefully in your hands rather than picking them up by a rim or handle. They are very fragile, and a foot or knob can be knocked off with one little tap. The bisque load may have two or three times as much ware as the glaze load. However, air does need to circulate through the ware to help burn out and remove gases. During the bisque firing, organic materials in the body (such as carbon and water) turn to gas and leave the ware. The open spaces which are left gradually disappear as glass begins to form and the body shrinks and becomes hard and strong. If the organic materials are not removed from the body, or are only partially removed, the trapped gases may try to push

through in the glaze firing and cause surface defects such as pinholes and bubbles. Also, if the carbon has not been fully removed from the body, the bisque may not become fully dense. This results in weaker ware that can more easily crack when heated in an oven or microwave or when washed in a dishwasher. Therefore, don't rush the bisque firing. Allow plenty of time for oxygen to move into the porous ware, especially before red heat (900°F or 482°C) and up to 1400°F (760°C). A downdraft vent helps to move air down through the kiln and remove fumes and gases, but if you don't have one, an open peephole can help, too. Thicker ware requires a longer firing than thin ware. A longer firing will also help the kiln shelves last longer.

Load the dry greenware into the kiln along with a Δ05 cone in the kiln sitter. Heat the kiln very slowly, keeping it under 200°F (93°C) for several hours, depending on the size and thickness of the pieces. I usually leave the lid propped open and one switch

A

B

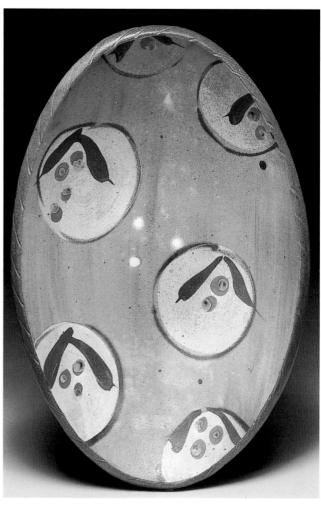

A
Erin Furimsky, *Cup*, 4½" × 5" × 3½" (11.4 × 12.7 × 8.9 cm), 1999.
Earthenware, slab, some coiling; terra sigillata, majolica, luster; bisque
Δ04, glaze Δ04, luster Δ18. Photo by Tyler Lotz

B
Will Ruggles and **Douglass Rankin**, *Oval Server*, 16½" × 11" × 3"
(41.9 × 27.9 × 7.6 cm), 1999. Stoneware, slab, decorated, draped and
compressed, plaster mold; slip background, slip circles, slip glazes; Δ9
wood-fired with salt and soda. Photo by Will Ruggles

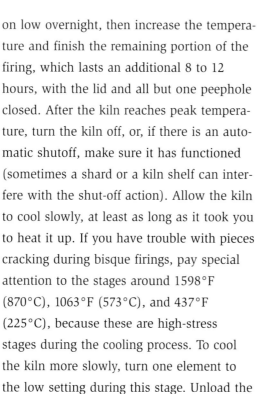

on low overnight, then increase the temperature and finish the remaining portion of the
firing, which lasts an additional 8 to 12
hours, with the lid and all but one peephole
closed. After the kiln reaches peak temperature, turn the kiln off, or, if there is an automatic shutoff, make sure it has functioned
(sometimes a shard or a kiln shelf can inter-
fere with the shut-off action). Allow the kiln
to cool slowly, at least as long as it took you
to heat it up. If you have trouble with pieces
cracking during bisque firings, pay special
attention to the stages around 1598°F
(870°C), 1063°F (573°C), and 437°F
(225°C), because these are high-stress
stages during the cooling process. To cool
the kiln more slowly, turn one element to
the low setting during this stage. Unload the

kiln when the ware is cool or below 300°F
(149°C).

If you have pieces ready for a glaze firing
that will be conducted at the same temperature as your bisque firing, you can combine
the two, as long as glazed pieces don't touch
other pieces. The longer firing won't hurt the
glazed pieces. Load the glazed ware
carefully, as the glaze coating is fragile and
can chip or rub off. If you're transporting
glazed ware to a kiln somewhere else, wrap
the work in plastic to protect the coating;
paper could rub the coating off.

Don't forget to place cone packs in front of
the peepholes (in addition to the cone in the
kiln sitter) as you load the ware. Check the

bottoms of all your pieces to make sure they are free of glaze, and leave a tiny bit of space between pieces in case they warp and want to fuse together. A small mirror will help you check to make sure that a shelf clears the top of the ware below. Large platters may need a bit of grog or silica sand under their feet to aid them in shrinking smoothly, but be careful to keep the grog from landing on the pieces below.

Tip

Mix fine grog or silica sand with wax resist, and brush this onto the feet of large platters to help them shrink smoothly on the kiln shelf and to keep the otherwise loose grit from filtering down onto pieces below.

You can stack pieces of broken kiln shelves on the kiln's stilts to vary the height of your shelving. Usually, you'll want to reserve the kiln's top shelf for taller pieces, find the flattest shelves for plates or platters (to keep them from warping), and fire lids in place on their pots (with the areas of the lid and pot that contact each other free of glaze). If, instead, you fire lids and their respective pots separately, position the pieces close to one another, in case there is some variation in temperature in the kiln (or in atmosphere if you're firing with a gas or wood-firing kiln).

Glaze Firing

A glaze firing can start out much faster than a bisque firing, especially if the pieces are not freshly glazed and still damp. Raise the temperature at a rate of 200° to 300°F (93° to 149°C) per hour. Again, a longer firing won't hurt. Once you've reached the final temperature, soak the kiln, or hold the temperature at an even level to allow the clay

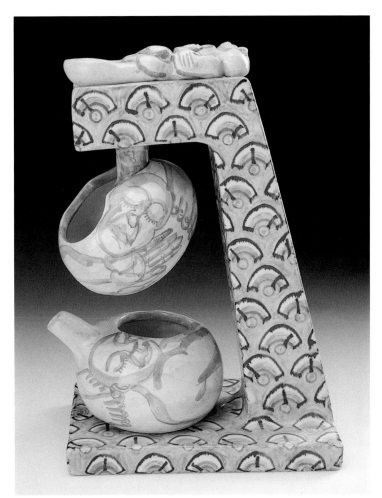

Marilyn Andrews, *Incubator*, 10½" x 7½" x 5" (26.7 x 19.1 x 12.7 cm), 1997. Slab-built stoneware; clay slip painting under clear matte glaze; Δ5 oxidation.
Photo by Jonathon Wallen

and glaze to mature. This will give bubbles or pinholes some time to smooth over. The peak temperature is more critical in a glaze firing, so pay close attention to your cone packs and pyrometer or controller.

Unloading a Kiln

Unloading the kiln is so exciting (it still is, even after decades!) that you will be tempted to rush the cooling or unload at scorching temperatures. You'll be cured after a beautiful piece cracks with a loud ping in your gloved hands! Wait until the temperature is below 300°F (149°C). With larger kilns, this could take two days, but usually 12 hours is sufficient.

Lisa R. Goldberg, *Black & White Serving Set*, 1999. Stoneware, slab; glazed, detail work with bulb syringe; Δ10 gas reduction. Photo by Mel Mittermiller

As you unload, take note of where glazes may appear to have gotten too hot or stayed too cool. In a fuel-burning kiln, reduction may have occurred in some places and not in others. Sometimes you can control how these variables affect your pieces by loading in a different way to change the circulation. In other situations, you may be able to take advantage of them by loading different glazes in different places in the kiln. If a piece has cracked, inspect it carefully. If glaze hasn't flowed over the edge and it is a clean, sharp crack, it may have been caused by a too-fast cooling. If the glaze has flowed over the edge, the crack occurred earlier in the firing, perhaps during a too-rapid heating. A record of your firing procedure will be helpful in solving problems with cracking or glaze flaws, so keep good notes. After a year of firing with my wood-burning kiln, I finally realized that my firing successes were related to the weather, and I figured out how to adjust my firings accordingly.

Following a glaze firing, check kiln shelves for glaze drips or shards, and grind these off so that when you brush off the shelf for the next firing, you don't cut your hand on a sharp fragment. Occasionally, an element will burn out in an electric kiln and either slow it down or stall the firing completely. Keep a spare set of elements on hand. They

are not difficult to change. Just make a note of where the wires go to replace them correctly. *Be sure to turn off the kiln and disconnect all power before working on it.* Even if the elements don't burn out, they may not heat as well with age, and you'll need to replace them after repeated firings. Several things can shorten their life: long soakings at high temperatures; contamination such as glaze, clay shards, or kiln wash on the element; tightly wound areas on the element coil resulting from improper stretching when replacing an element; firings in which pieces or shelves were too close to an element. The element groove can be vacuumed to keep it free of debris.

Glazing

When you're making tableware, glazing is not just an embellishment but also an hygienic concern. Glazes make the ware smooth and easier to clean. After struggling to nurture your ware through all the construction processes, it may be frustrating to learn that this will be one more essential skill to master. Actually, the process of glazing will be easier if you view it not as embellishment or an afterthought, but as an action contemplated right from the beginning of the design and construction of the piece. The glaze should complement, not overwhelm, the object, whether it involves a colorful pattern or one simple color.

And you've got lots of details to consider. How will food look on the piece once it's glazed? Does the glaze you have in mind scratch or chip easily? Will it crack in a network of fine lines over time? How does it look on different kinds of clay? Is consistency a concern in order to match different pieces in a place setting? Will the sound of a fork over a matte glaze be grating? In addition to thinking through questions like these, you'll want to choose your glaze based on your firing temperature, your clay, and your kiln.

Two types of glaze firings are possible: oxidation or reduction. An oxidation firing is the type that goes on in electric kilns. In a reduction firing, the kiln atmosphere, during strategic periods, is deprived of oxygen, and as a result, the colors of clay and glazes are changed in a particular way. A brown clay may turn warmer in tone and cause speckles in the glaze, and a glaze with copper could turn red instead of the usual oxidation green. The ancient Chinese celadon greens and blues, which derived their color from iron, were formerly possible only in reduction firings, though that has recently changed. Reduction firing requires a fuel-burning kiln so that the fuel-to-air ratio can be controlled. You can also do an oxidation firing in a fuel-burning kiln, though it is a little more difficult with wood than it is with gas.

Rosemarie Stadnyk, *Etched in Blue,* 5⅜" × 3¼" × 9" (13.5 × 8.5 × 23 cm), 1999. Stoneware, pressed slabs, coils; impressed design from plaster mold, glaze; Δ6 oxidation. Photo by Menno Fieguth

Both glaze formulas and commercial glazes typically specify the type of firing for which they are best suited and the cone number at which they mature. They also specify their surface characteristic, such as matte, shiny, textured, colored, and so on. Glaze additives, or gums, now on the market help make a tougher coating and are very helpful when added to sprayed glazes. They're already a part of the formula in commercial glazes.

The most important consideration for tableware is whether the glaze is food safe. Don't use any glazes containing lead or barium. Commercial glazes should be marked non-lead and tableware safe. If you are mixing your own glazes, contact a testing lab to have them tested if you are unsure what the latest research says about the ingredients. You should avoid (or certainly test) glaze formulas that contain large amounts of chrome, cobalt, selenium, cadmium, vanadium, lithium, or manganese dioxide.

Another important consideration for a tableware glaze is *fit*. A glaze must be chosen to match the shrinkage rate of the particular clay body on which it is to be used, or the glaze may craze or shiver.

Crazing is a network of fine cracks in a fired glaze, owing to different rates of expansion and contraction between the glaze and the clay. Changing or altering the clay body may solve the problem, but it may be easier to alter the glaze, if you mix your own. If you're running into problems, try altering your glaze as follows: increase the silica, decrease the feldspar, add small amounts of talc, increase the clay content, increase the boron, or decrease any material with sodium or potassium.

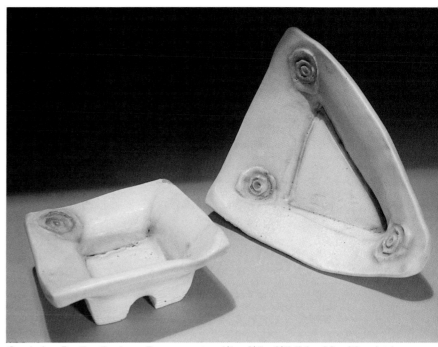

Carole Ann Fer, *Two Condiment Trays*, square tray 1½" × 3½" × 3½" (3.8 × 8.9 × 8.9 cm), triangle tray 1½" × 7" × 4½" (3.8 × 17.8 × 11.4 cm), 1999. Porcelain, slump mold; clay stamp applied, copper slip washed off; Δ6 oxidation. Photo by Ellen Wieske

Shivering is the reverse of crazing. Shivering occurs when a glaze is too compressed, which causes it to separate from the clay and peel or shiver, breaking off in small flakes. This is frequently due to the clay shrinking more than the glaze. Usually, shivering can be remedied by decreasing the flint in the glaze and increasing the feldspar or other alkali-bearing materials. Sometimes, a glaze under compression may break the ware, especially if the walls of the pot are very thin and the glaze is thick. This is most likely to occur if the glaze is very thick on the inside of the piece and is applied thinly, or not at all, on the outside. A flat baking dish, for example, may need to be glazed on the underside, inside of the foot rim or feet, to help prevent shivering.

GLAZE TYPES AND SURFACE DECORATIONS SUITABLE FOR TABLEWARE

Crystalline glazes. The crystalline pattern that these glazes develop is caused by certain ingredients (zinc, borax, or potassium, for example) and by the manner in which the kiln is cooled during firing.

Ash glazes. These glazes were probably discovered when a potter first noticed that ash on the shoulders of pots removed from a wood-fired kiln had melted to form a glassy surface. They're used in both oxidation and reduction firings and are made by washing ashes and adding them to high-fire glazes.

Salt and soda glazes. High-fired salt and soda glazes form a glassy coating with an orange-peel texture by introducing sodium chloride into the hot kiln chamber. Since the fumes are toxic, potters have recently switched to soda firings, which use sodium bicarbonate.

Slip glazes. Commonly used by early American stoneware potters, these are glazes made from clays that contain natural fluxes. Because they're made from clay, slip glazes must match the clay body to which they're applied in terms of shrinkage.

Majolica glazes. These tin glazes are historically associated with Spain. The term refers to a style in which earthenware clay is glazed with a white, tin-opacified, viscous glaze, then decorated with colored brushwork and fired to a low temperature.

Overglazes. A colored glaze design to be applied over another glaze is an overglaze. Overglazes include enamels, china paints, and lusters; all can be applied either after a piece is glazed but before it is fired, or, more often, on top of a fired glaze. In the latter case, you'll return the piece to the kiln for a low-temperature firing. Luster glazes are sometimes used without another glaze under them, but with their large amount of metal, they are not considered safe for tableware when they cover large areas.

Underglazes. The name confuses a lot of people, because underglazes are sometimes used on top of an unfired glaze, as in majolica, to provide different colors. They can be mixed in the studio or purchased in a variety of forms, including liquids, chalks, pencils, or tubes. They provide a flat color by themselves and a brighter hue under or over a clear glaze.

Slips. A slip is composed of clay and water, usually held in suspension with a deflocculant like sodium silicate, and is used to color the surface of a pot, or, as in slip trailing, to provide a textured decoration. Some slips are

Jenny Lou Sherburne, *Cornucopia Fruit Bowl Set,* 20" × 30" × 15" (50.8 × 76.2 × 38.1 cm), 1998. Slab-built stoneware, coiled, pinched, clay additions; carved and pinched with engobes and glazes; Δ06 and Δ04. Photo by Steve Meltzer

A

B

C

D

A
Gail Price, *Trophy Trout* (serving platter), 4¼" × 23" × 15" (10.8 × 58.4 × 38.1 cm), 2000. Stoneware, slab, carved, textured; glaze, wax resist; Δ8 oxidation. Photo by David O. Marlow

B
Erin Furimsky, *Platter*, 8½" × 11" × 1½" (21.6 × 27.9 × 3.8 cm), 1999. Earthenware, press-mold front, back built up; terra sigillata, majolica, luster, white slip with carving; bisque Δ04, glaze Δ04, luster Δ18. Photo by Tyler Lotz

C
Shay Amber, *Nature's Fire*, 11" × 2" (27.9 × 5.1 cm), 2000. Earthenware, slab and coil; adorned with hand-carved impressions, oxide washes, several layers of underglaze; Δ04. Photo by Neil Pickett

D
Renee Baltzell, *Butterdish*, 4¼" × 8⅛" × 4¾" (10.8 × 20.6 × 12.1 cm), 1999. Slab, pinched low-fire white clay; underglazes, engobe, glaze; Δ04 to Δ06 oxidation. Photo by Lew Baltzell

A

A

Kathy King, *Flirtation*, 6" × 11" × 5"
(15.2 × 27.9 × 12.7 cm), 2000.
Midrange porcelain, handbuilt slab
stand, sugar and creamer have
thrown and altered bodies, handbuilt
finial on lids, slab spout on creamer;
sgraffito, underglaze, transparent
glazes, china paint firings; Δ6 oxidation. Photo by artist

B

Marko Fields, *Biomorphic Deviled Egg
Platter*, 11" × 14" × 1" (27.9 × 35.6 ×
2.5 cm), 2000. Porcelain, slab, carved,
molded; incising and sgraffito through
underglazes; Δ6 oxidation. Photo by
artist and Darren Whitley

C

Jenny Mendes, *Striped Salt and Pepper Shakers*, 6" × 2½" × 2½" (15.2 ×
6.4 × 6.4 cm), 1998. Terra-cotta, coil;
painted terra sigillata underglazes; Δ2.
Photo by David Kingsbury

B

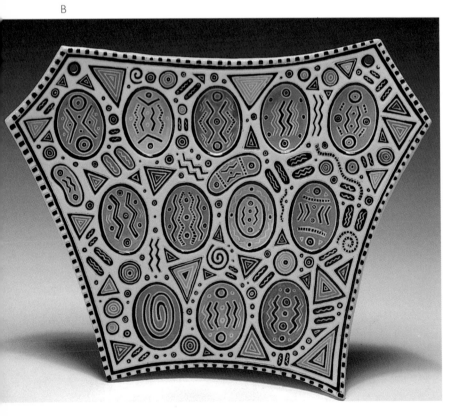

C

formulated for bisqueware and greenware, others only for one or the other. Slips are sometimes colored with oxides or stains.

Engobes. Applied to greenware or bisqueware, engobes are similar to clay slips, but include flint, feldspar, and fluxes to make them melt and shrink to fit the clay body to which they're applied. They may also be colored with oxides or stains.

Metallic colorants. Metallic colorants, which are added in small amounts to glazes, slips, and engobes, include iron, cobalt, copper, chrome, manganese, nickel, and other metals. They can be mixed with water and sprayed, brushed, or sponged on and then covered with a glaze. Use gloves and a respirator when handling them.

Stains. To create stains, metallic colorants are mixed with other ingredients that help regulate the mixture's color, quality of melt, and ease of application. Stains come in powdered form in a wide variety of colors. You can add them to glazes and clays to color them, or you can mix them with other ingredients to make underglazes. The process is similar to, for example, adding cobalt oxide to a glaze to make it blue, but because the stains are finely ground, you don't end up with a blue speckled effect.

BUYING READY-MADE GLAZES OR MIXING YOUR OWN

The range of colors, surface finishes, and required firing temperatures you'll find in commercially prepared glazes is enormous. Many professional potters prefer buying ready-made glazes from suppliers rather than mixing and screening their own and storing all the necessary raw materials. On the other

hand, many others love experimenting with the thousands of glaze formulas available. They can use them to create an even wider range of glaze choices for themselves and to come up with a unique look of their own—and do so cheaply. The reason I like mixing my own is because I learn what the different ingredients do in the glaze, and therefore I can figure out how to change the glaze to suit my artistic intent. After you have experimented, you will learn that changing the firing temperature a cone or two or increasing or reducing the matte quality or shininess of a glaze is not so hard. There are numerous excellent books on understanding glazes, so I won't go further except to say that a chemistry degree is not a prerequisite for playing with glazes—just take careful notes!

Robin Campo and Patricia Guerra, *New Tea*, 6" × 4" × 8" (15.2 × 10.2 × 20.3 cm), 1999. Earthenware, cast, assembled, handbuilt; multi-fired china paints and lusters; Δ05 and Δ018 oxidation. Photo by Robin Campo

TESTING GLAZES

I still get excited taking glaze tests out of the kiln, because the results are always surprising. The best formulas to test are those from other potters. If you're just starting, find formulas that call for the most basic ingredients; it's hard to get a good idea what quantities you'll want to buy in bulk later before you've mixed a few different formulas. To test them, mix them first in small batches, 100 to 200 grams, and try them on small tiles of different clays in both thick and thin applications. Make some of your test tiles with textures,

Glaze tests

too, to see how the glaze performs over texture. Above all, resist the urge to test what sounds like a great glaze on your best piece! The photo above shows the results of numerous glaze tests I've conducted over the years.

MIXING GLAZES

Determine your batch size and make sure you have the right amount of all the ingredients and the right size container. Two hundred grams of dry ingredients will make about 1 cup (.24 L) of glaze. One thousand grams will fit into a 1-gallon (3.8 L) bucket, and 10,000 grams will fit into a 5-gallon (19 L) bucket.

Wear your respirator and weigh each ingredient, checking each off as you go. Dry mix the materials and add water. The formulas never say how much water, so err on the low side; you can always add more, but you can't take it out. Some potters like to let this mixture slake a few hours before stirring it, to allow the lumps to soften. Others immediately mix it with a stick, spatula, or a drill with a mixer attachment. Glazes are usually mixed with enough water to form the consistency of thick cream. The oxide solutions for brushwork or spraying are thinner. Commercial glaze *hydrometers* (which are dropped gently into the mixture to see at what level they float) do not tell you how thick to

Using a hydrometer

make a glaze, but will help you to make it the same each time. Sieve the mixed glaze, then add more water to get the consistency you want. I sieve first through a coarse utility strainer, then sieve it back into my container with a 60-mesh strainer, and this seems to quicken the process a bit. Sometimes, getting the thickness correct will be frustratingly variable and will depend on the type of clay the glaze is to be used on. Each glaze will be a little different. I mark each glaze bucket with a number that corresponds to a number on the correct level on the hydrometer, once I determine how thick I like the glaze. After glaze sits in a bucket for a period of time, you'll probably need to add more water to compensate for what evaporates.

A
Susan Kay Wechsler, *Frog & Lily Pad Bread/Hors d'oeuvres Plate,* 18" × 7" × 1½" (45.7 × 17.8 × 3.8 cm), 1999. Stoneware and porcelain slip, slab, layered; clear glaze; Δ5 oxidation. Photo by Russ Russo

B
Krystal Wick, *Chip and Dip Set,* platter 15" (38.1 cm) wide, cup 5" × 2" (12.7 × 5 cm), 1999. White dover clay, built on mold; penciled, underglazed, glazed; Δ04.
Photo by James R. Plagmann

C
Susan Kay Wechsler, *Woven Fall Red Oak Bread Basket,* 4" × 12" × 12" (10.2 × 30.5 × 30.5 cm), 1999. Stoneware, handwoven with rolled textured coils, braided rim; applique of cast and pressed leaves and acorns, oxide stained; Δ5 oxidation. Photo by Russ Russo

D
Barbara Glynn Prodaniuk, *Bear Spirit Box (salt cellar),* 10½" × 3" × 5" (26.7 × 7.6 × 12.7 cm), 1999. Stoneware, slab, pinched, sculpted, carved; carved, partial glazing; Δ06 bisque, Δ06 raku with post-firing reduction.
Photo by Orest Prodanink

A

Renee Baltzell, *Butterdish,* 4¼" × 8⅛" × 4¾" (10.8 × 20.6 × 12.1 cm), 1999. Slab, pinched low-fire white clay; underglazes, engobe, glaze; Δ04 to Δ06 oxidation. Photo by Lew Baltzell

B

Kathy Steinsberger, *Blueberries are Heaven-Sent!,* 3" × 14" × 14" (7.6 × 35.6 × 35.6 cm), 1999. Earthenware, slab, paddled, smoothed with tennis ball, handles pulled; underglazes and clear glaze; Δ04 and Δ05. Photo by Doug Van Zandt

C

Rina Peleg, *Handwoven Ceramic Baskets,* 18" × 11" × 4" (45.7 × 27.9 × 10.2 cm),1990-2000. Terra-cotta white earthenware, extruded coil, handwoven; underglaze and clear glaze; Δ04. Photo by artist

A

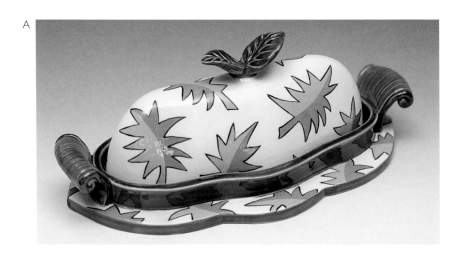

B

C

APPLYING GLAZES

Potters are usually generous in sharing their glaze recipes. One reason may be that they know the most beautiful glazes in the world will depend more on skill of application than on the formula—another reason to make LOTS of pots so you can practice different ways of applying glaze. The clay will make a difference in how the glaze looks, even with an opaque glaze. The thickness or thinness of application will also make a difference. An uneven application will be more apparent with a matte glaze than with a shiny glaze. Glaze application can involve several steps with various layers of stains, resists, oxides, carving through layers of engobes, and repeated firings at different temperatures. I can't go into full details of all of the techniques here (as I mentioned earlier, there are plenty of books devoted to the subject of glazing alone), but here's a brief explanation of the major application methods. Experiment with as many as you can at first to get a feeling for which one best fits your work style.

Brushing

Brushing is a good method when you have only a small amount of glaze to work with. It is slow and can yield uneven results unless you use several thin layers rather than one thick one. Ceramic gums (which are already in commercial glazes) help the glaze to brush on more fluidly. You mix them with hot water first, then add them to the glaze mixture. If you're using a brush to apply an underglaze, you'll want to practice your brushwork, so the flow of the strokes shows deliberation or spontaneity or precision—whatever your goal. Practice on paper first to alleviate hesitancy that might appear as awkwardness once you move to your piece.

Trailing

Plastic squeeze bottles filled with engobe or glaze can be used to draw squiggle lines, to squirt glaze across a pot, or to apply one glaze on top of another. A *deflocculated* clay slip or an engobe can be trailed on greenware to create textured designs.

Pouring

Pouring is used to glaze the interiors of pieces. You allow the glaze to roll around the inside, then pour it out, completing the process before glazing the outside. Pouring can be used for exteriors, too, especially if a piece is too large to be dipped in the glaze container. Hold the piece upside down over the glaze bucket or set it on a couple of

Brushing underglaze

Glazing the interior of a piece

sticks that span the container. Using a dipper (I use plastic measuring cups with handles), pour the glaze over the outside of the piece. Turn the piece upright after the glaze stops dripping and is dry enough to handle.

Dipping

Holding a piece by the foot and dipping it in the glaze is the easiest way to obtain an even coverage. You can use glaze tongs for those pieces that are awkward to hold. Dishpans and big mixing bowls are handy to have if your glaze bucket isn't wide enough to accommodate the piece you're dipping. The only drawback to dipping is having to have a large quantity of glaze mixed.

Dipping a piece to glaze it

Spraying

Spraying is a good solution for glazing large pieces and for obtaining an even coverage. It is also a good choice for times when handling a piece would put an underglaze decoration in danger of smearing or when a fired piece has glaze flaws and needs another glaze application and firing. In this case, heating the piece first will help the glaze dry more quickly. Oxides and underglazes can be sprayed with an airbrush or small spray gun.

Use a turntable in the spray booth to keep the piece moving so you're not overspraying one area. Experience will tell you how thickly to spray. Some potters make a little pencil mark on the piece and know they've sprayed enough when the mark is covered. The sprayed glaze coating will appear thicker than a dipped coating, and it's more fragile in the raw state. You can add ceramic gums to the glaze mixture to make it tougher.

Resists

Masking tape, wax resist, and liquid latex are some of the materials you can use on bisque-ware for resist effects. Water-based liquid wax resist is usually used on foot rims to keep glaze from adhering there. Allow it to dry for an hour to form a good resist. You can also use it on greenware or on top of a glaze before applying a contrasting glaze. Be careful not to accidently drip it on areas where you want glaze to stick. If this happens, you can scrub it off with a wet sponge or sandpaper or burn it off with a small propane torch or in the kiln.

A Few Glazing Tips

■ Before glazing, use a brush or an air compressor to dust off your pieces. Some potters prefer to dip each piece quickly in a bucket of clean water. Don't wash them too long, however, or the pieces will become too saturated with water to pick up an adequate glaze coat, especially on thin areas.

■ Any area that touches the kiln shelf must be free of glaze.

■ If you're firing a lid in place, wax the lid rim and the area where it rests on the pot. If your lids prove to be difficult

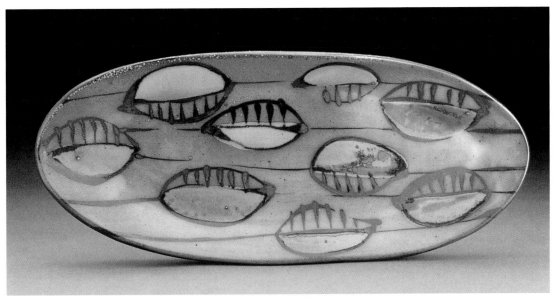

Suze Lindsay, *Oval Platter,* 1" × 10" × 4½" (2.5 × 25.4 × 11.4 cm), 1999. Slab-built stoneware; slip and glaze brushwork; Δ10 salt firing. Photo by Tom Mills

to remove after firing, add a teaspoon of alumina hydrate to a cup of wax resist, and brush it on the lid rims and resting areas for subsequent firings. It will leave a fine powder on those contact areas, but you can brush off the residue after the firing. Just remember not to mistake this altered wax solution for pure wax you want to use as a resist on top of a glaze.

■ Always stir your glaze thoroughly just before using it.

■ When overlapping glazes, make sure the thicker overlapped area is not too close to the foot of your piece; thicker areas can run.

■ If a glaze coating cracks as it dries, it may be too thick and could peel off in areas. This is called *crawling*. You can scrape off the problem glaze and wash the pot, just be sure to dry it well before glazing again. Sometimes dried glaze drips can also be shaved down with a sharp knife.

■ Glaze can be used to adhere a knob to a lid on top of a pot—one that has been popped off or purposely made separately, so it can be glazed a different color. Mix the glaze with a little white glue, which helps hold the added piece on while you're loading it into the kiln. (Note that this technique is only useful for adding small pieces. It won't work for adding a handle to the side of a cup, for example).

■ If a glazed plate bottom is dangerously close to the kiln shelf and could sag and stick, leave a little unglazed circle on the bottom and place a wad of clay there as a temporary firing support. I had to do this on the plates in the Spicy Harvest Setting on page 50 and the Spring Tea Setting on page 76.

■ Remember to take notes on what glaze technique you used on which pieces and on your test tiles. Nothing is more frustrating than unloading a fabulous piece and not remembering how to create the same look again!

CHAPTER 2

SPICY HARVEST SETTING

LAYING A SLAB OF CLAY over a "hump" mold is the simplest way I've found yet to make a plate. The method is also a lot of fun, because the plate silhouette can be any shape you like. I've chosen a modified square, but an asymmetrical shape would work, too. The bowl in this set is constructed out of four joined stiff slabs, but it could just as easily be a single slab draped over a mold. Your mold can be one you've made of clay and then bisque fired, or it can be a found object. I've used glass light-fixture shades, plastic or metal disc snow sleds, metal mixing bowls, woks, and even hubcaps and pillows for molds. Thrift stores and hardware stores are good places to search for objects that are just the right shape. Some potters also make their molds by casting plaster in bowls. Plaster or bisque-fired clay molds permit the clay slab to be draped directly over them, but a nonporous mold (a metal bowl, for example) would need to be covered with plastic or fabric to keep the clay from sticking to it. If you modify the shape of your mold by adding clay (maybe to build up one part of the mold), be sure to use two layers of plastic over it before you lay your slab on top, or the slab will be difficult to remove.

For this set's extruded tumbler, I chose a standard hexagonal die, because I liked the way the geometry of the faceted sides worked with the geometry of the plates. The pitcher requires a larger version of the same hexagonal die, combined with a slab and other elements. You can imagine that if you were to design your own dies, the possibilities for shapes would be endless. The clay I have chosen is a red earthenware that will fire to △03 (2014°F or 1101°C). I liked the look of the way this brown clay reacts with the glaze to show the surface texture. The areas that will not be covered with glaze will end up a warm red-brown color after the final firing.

Materials and Tools

- ▲ Poster board
- ▲ Scissors
- ▲ Pen or pencil
- ▲ Ruler
- ▲ 25 lbs. (11.35 kg) red earthenware for Δ 03 oxidation firing (per place setting)
- ▲ Cutting wire
- ▲ Rolling pin, wooden dowel, or slab roller
- ▲ Canvas
- ▲ Several ware boards
- ▲ Knife
- ▲ Pieces to use as molds
- ▲ Plastic (Old dry-cleaning bags are perfect; for covering molds, you can also use a thin fabric such as muslin.)

- ▲ Pony roller (optional)
- ▲ Scoring tool
- ▲ Needle tool
- ▲ Slip
- ▲ Several brushes
- ▲ Wooden modeling tool (optional)
- ▲ Wooden paddle or stick
- ▲ Wooden or rubber rib
- ▲ Sponge
- ▲ Extruder and dies for tumblers and pitcher (optional)
- ▲ Length of foam pipe insulation (optional)
- ▲ Texturizing materials or tools (optional)
- ▲ Wax resist

- ▲ Black underglaze for signing pieces (optional) (You can either buy a commercial underglaze or add black stain to the underglaze formula in Appendix D.)
- ▲ Compressed air (optional)
- ▲ 4 gallons (15.2 L) Δ03 Blue Satin Glaze (See Appendix D for formula.)
- ▲ Bucket large enough for dipping platter
- ▲ Glaze hydrometer (optional)

Starting Tip

- ▲ If you don't have an extruder, consider adapting the slab cup design in Chapter 5 (beginning on page 90) for your pitcher base and for cups for this place setting.

PLATE STEPS

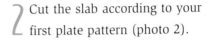

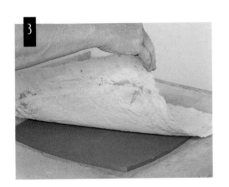

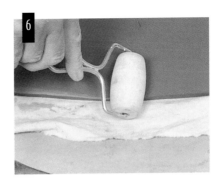

1 Start by making some cardboard patterns for the size and shape plates you want, taking into consideration clay shrinkage. (See page 13 for calculating shrinkage.) Roll out a slab of clay approximately ¼ inch (6 mm) thick (photo 1).

2 Cut the slab according to your first plate pattern (photo 2).

3 If your mold is non-porous, cover it with plastic or a thin fabric such as muslin. Lay the slab over the mold, centering it by adjusting the plastic or fabric. If you have a problem laying the slab on top of the mold without distorting the slab, try this: with the slab on a piece of canvas or a board, place the fabric on the slab, add the mold on top of that, and then flip the entire sandwich over (photos 3-5).

4 Lightly smooth the edges of the plate with a wooden paddle, stick, or a pony roller, or just use your finger (photo 6).

5 Score the places where the feet will go (photo 7). No, you don't *have* to have feet, but they do seem to give the plate a more elegant feel when you set it on a table. Feet will also allow you to glaze more of the bottom of the plate. To make the feet, roll out four small coils of clay and press them onto the scored areas (photo 8). Usually, it isn't neces-

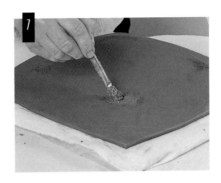

sary to score a join when the clay is soft, but feet are vulnerable to being popped off in handling, so it's a good idea to take the extra precaution. Rest a board on the feet to level them. (One drawback to four feet is that they could prevent the plate from sitting perfectly level. As an alternative, you could consider three feet, or perhaps a foot rim cut from a slab.)

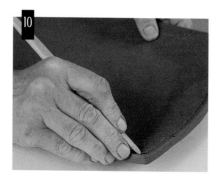

BOWL STEPS

6 Scribe your signature on the bottom with a needle tool (photo 9), or wait until glazing time and use an underglaze to sign your name.

7 Allow it to dry slowly to the leather-hard stage, then remove the plate from the mold and smooth the inner edge of the rim with your finger or a damp sponge. You may also want to use a wooden modeling tool or dull pencil to scribe a few lines just inside the rim, merely to add some visual interest (photo 10). Use other patterns and repeat steps 1 through 7 to make plates of other sizes for your set, if you like.

After experimenting with several different shapes of cardboard templates, I decided to make a bowl of four identical slab shapes. You may find it helpful to make a cardboard bowl first to help you determine the size and shape you want. Of course, as an alternative, you could drape a soft slab over an appropriate mold and paddle and shape it to make it conform. But one note of caution if you go that route: remove the clay from the mold before it shrinks too much, or cracking could occur.

1 Create your template pieces. Roll out a slab of clay, approximately ¼ inch (6 mm) thick, and allow it to stiffen to leather hard before cutting out the four shapes.

Save a small piece of the slab for the bottom. As you cut the pieces, bevel the edges that will be joined (photo 11).

2 Gently shape the pieces with a slight curve, if you like (photo 12).

3 Score the edges, apply slip with a brush, and press the edges firmly together (photo 13). You may find it easier to join the pieces by forming the bowl upside down.

4 Paddle the joins and smooth them with a rib to make the bowl stronger and smoother (photo 14).

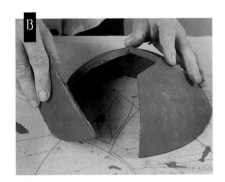

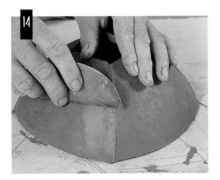

5 Roll out four small coils of clay and press one into each join inside the bowl to strengthen them (photo 15). Smooth the joins with your fingers or a sponge.

6 Score the bottom edges of the four joined slabs and then score a corresponding shape on the piece of the slab you saved for the bottom of the bowl. Apply slip, join the two together, and cut out the bottom (photo 16). Again, add a coil around this join (inside the bowl) to strengthen it.

7 Trim any excess clay from the base (photo 17), and paddle and sponge as necessary to smooth the bond.

8 Add small coil feet to the bottom of the bowl, scoring and applying slip to attach them (photo 18). Level the feet with a board, or simply position the bowl upright on a flat surface. Smooth the rim of the bowl, so there are no sharp edges. Be wary of using the wet sponge too much as you do so; sometimes excessive sponging can leave the clay edge feeling gritty, as the small particles of clay are washed away and larger ones remain on the surface. Allow the bowl to dry slowly.

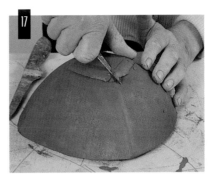

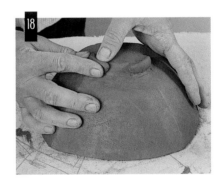

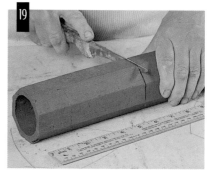

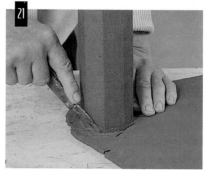

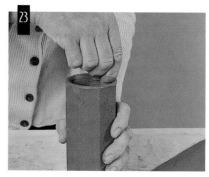

1 After you have chosen and positioned the die on the extruder, slice off blocks of clay to fit the extruder barrel, and extrude clay for your tumblers. You can make your extrusions any length; simply continue loading clay into the barrel to lengthen them. I usually cut off extrusions to roughly correspond to the length of my ware boards, which are about 2 feet (61 cm) long. Straighten any curves before the extrusions dry (unless curves are what you want).

2 Make a slab ¼ inch (6 mm) thick; you'll cut pieces from this slab to form the bottoms of your tumblers. Allow both the extrusions and the slab to dry. When they're equally leather hard, cut the extrusions into sections for your tumblers (photo 19). (I cut mine approximately 6 inches [15.2 cm] long.)

3 To form a bottom on a tumbler, score the lower edge of the tumbler, score a corresponding area on the slab, and apply

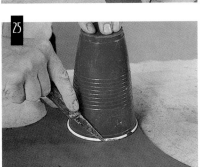

slip (photo 20). Firmly press the tube onto the slab, and slice off the excess clay from around the base by angling the knife slightly to form a bevel (photo 21). This will give a slight lift to the look of the form, so it's less clunky.

4 Smooth the edge of each tumbler with the paddle (photo 22), and smooth each rim with a wet finger, gently rounding it so it turns out slightly, to make pouring easier (photo 23).

5 With the brush, apply slip to smooth the seam on the inside of each tumbler (photo 24). If your hand will fit inside, add a coil to each seam. It is important that the inside be smooth and easy to clean.

6 You can easily turn one of your tumblers into a matching kitchen storage container by adding a lid. Simply make a slab or coil flange to add to a slab disc (photos 25-27), and then attach a creative knob (photos 28 and 29). You'll ensure the best fit if you make the lid at the same time you make the container. That way, shrinkage of the two items will be at the same stage. For other variations, consider adding handles (see pages 102 and 103 for lots of options) or even a loop on the side for holding a wooden spoon, as for a mustard jar.

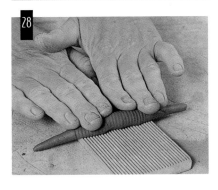

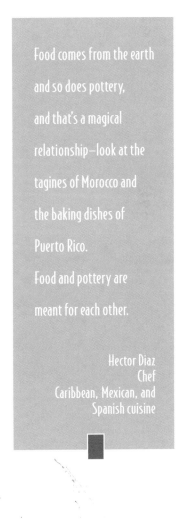

Food comes from the earth and so does pottery, and that's a magical relationship—look at the tagines of Morocco and the baking dishes of Puerto Rico. Food and pottery are meant for each other.

Hector Diaz
Chef
Caribbean, Mexican, and
Spanish cuisine

A pitcher is an interesting project because it is composed of different elements (body, handle, spout, base), and all the elements must work together if the pitcher is to function with balance and stability. The handle will need to comfortably accommodate a hand and be strong enough to lift the vessel once it's full of liquid. Only experience (and the study of successful and unsuccessful pitchers you've made) can help you figure out exactly where a pitcher handle should be placed. (You shouldn't lift a fragile, unfired pitcher by the handle to determine whether you've got it right. Wait until it's fired, then fill it with liquid and give it a try.) You can also get some help from examining others' pitchers and jugs for inspiration.

The spout should enable the pitcher to pour liquid without causing it to dribble down the side. An exaggerated spout, one in which the spout's edge is above the rim of the pot, will help your pitcher's pouring ability. So will a sharp edge on the bottom of the pouring lip. A full-bodied throat will also help guide liquid smoothly out of the vessel (rather than down the side and onto the tablecloth).

1 Choose an extruder die that matches or complements the tumblers, but that has a larger diameter. If you want your pitcher base to feature a substantial curve, bend the extrusion while it is still soft. (You can still make smaller changes in the curve after it has stiffened somewhat.) One way to curve your pitcher base is to extrude it onto foam pipe insulation, then use the pipe to bend the extrusion and keep it from collapsing (photo 30).

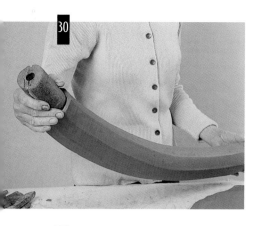

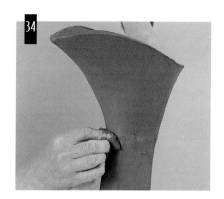

2 Roll out a slab ¼" (6 mm) thick, and allow it to dry and stiffen along with the extrusion. Meantime, experiment with cardboard shapes to figure out what shape will make a pitcher spout that might pour well and look good to you (photo 31).

3 Once the extrusion and the slab are leather hard, cut out the shapes you've decided on for the spout, and bend them to fit (photo 32).

Tip

When forming a slab into a tight curve, do so in the soft-clay stage, then place it over a wad of paper or plastic to let it stiffen before you work with it. If you try to bend it when it's too stiff, it could crack.

4 Join the slabs of the spout by scoring, applying slip, and paddling, then score and apply slip to attach the spout to the base, and smooth the join with a wet sponge (photos 33 and 34).

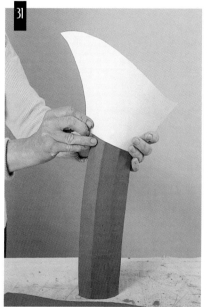

5 Smooth the rim of the spout, and use a wet finger to form a nice lip for pouring (photo 35).

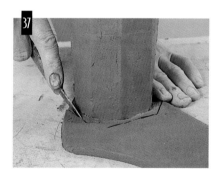

6 Add a small coil to the join to define the separation between the forms and to strengthen the join (photo 36).

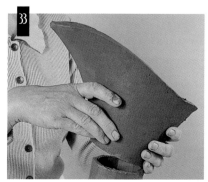

7 Score the pitcher's bottom edge, score a corresponding shape on

the slab, and press the two firmly together. Be sure to consider the stability of the pitcher at this point. Perhaps, rather than beveling this lower edge in, as you did on the tumbler, you'll want to make the base larger than the cylinder (photo 37).

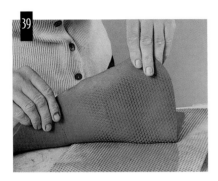

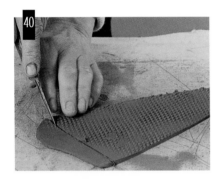

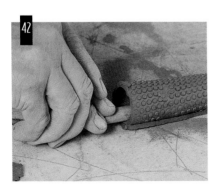

8 Carefully smooth the seam on the inside of the cylinder, and add a coil to the seam if your hand will fit inside. A crevice-free interior is important to keeping the inside of the pitcher clean once you begin putting it to use. Add a coil around the area where the bottom of the cylinder and the base meet to strengthen this join (photo 38).

9 For the handle, roll out a thin, ⅛-inch (3 mm) slab. If you like, texturize this piece; I used a piece of perforated metal material to texturize mine (photo 39). You can find numerous objects to create interesting textures, from natural found objects to industrial cast-off materials. Or, you can make marks on a clay slab, bisque fire it, and press pieces of clay into it to texturize them.

Tip

If the clay tends to stick to your texturizing material, try spraying the material with a spray lubricant or a spray cooking oil.

10 Cut a wedge shape out of the slab, and carefully form the textured wedge into a tube over a brush handle or a wooden dowel (photos 40 and 41).

11 Gently press the edges of the tube together to firm the seam by pressing from the inside with a dowel (photo 42).

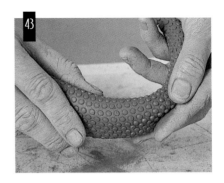

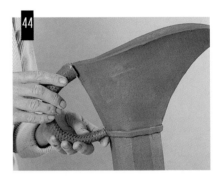

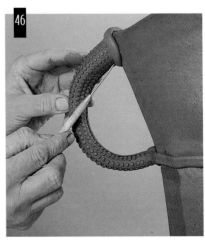

12 Carefully bend the piece into a curved handle shape (photo 43). I say carefully, because it is easy to mar the texture. Practice making several handles in different sizes and shapes. Then, when one cracks or gets mushy and loses its fresh, crisp texture, you can pick another. Allow the handles to dry to the same degree as the other pitcher parts, remembering that small parts dry faster than larger, thicker ones.

13 Score the handle and the spot where it will go, apply slip, and firmly join it to the pitcher (photo 44).

14 To strengthen this join, add a small coil or a few small discs of clay pressed firmly into the join (photo 45).

15 With the needle tool, add a small pinhole to the handle to allow trapped air to escape from the hollow piece during firing (photo 46).

16 Cover the piece with plastic and allow it to dry slowly.

EXTRUDED SERVING BOWL STEPS

Just as you did for this set's pitcher, you can either choose a manufactured die for your extruded serving bowl or you can make your own. Purchased dies typically come in standard, simple shapes. If you want something more unusual, marine-grade plywood is a good material for making your own. Also, metal laser-cutting businesses can quickly make precision cuts in metal plates to your specifications.

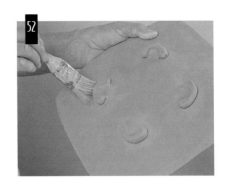

1 Choose or make your die and extrude your piece. I decided to make an extruder die that would incorporate a foot rim (photo 47).

2 After the extrusion has stiffened, cut a wedge-shaped piece of clay out of the middle of both ends (photo 48).

3 Score the cut edges, apply slip, bend the sides around, and join them together (photo 49).

4 Make handles for each end by simply rolling out a solid tube of clay, texturizing it if you like, and then coiling it. Score the handles and the spots where you'll attach them, apply slip, and join the handles firmly to the bowl, adding a small disc of clay to strengthen the join on each side (photos 50 and 51). Dry the bowl slowly on a flat surface.

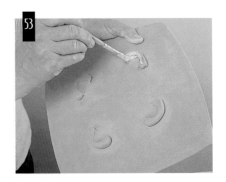

GLAZING STEPS

After you've bisque fired your pieces, you're ready to glaze them. I chose a blue semi-matte glaze because I like the way it shows a difference between a thick and thin application when I overlap two layers of the glaze in the dipping process. Dipping a piece into a bucket of glaze is a good way to achieve an even glaze coverage. The only disadvantage is that you need a big bucket of glaze.

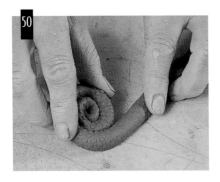

1 Brush off any dust from the bisque-fired pieces (photo 52). Be sure to check the inside of the vessels for any small pieces of debris. You can use a clean brush or compressed air for this step.

2 With a small brush, apply wax resist to the feet of the plates and bowls, to the bottoms of the other pieces, and to any part of any object that will touch the kiln shelf or come very close to touching the kiln shelf (photo 53). Usually, leaving a 1/4-inch (6 mm) margin is safe. Allow the resist to dry.

Tip

If you find that your plates are slumping in the glaze firing and sticking to the kiln shelf, you can wax a circle in the center of the bottom side of your plates and place a small disc of clay there. Pop the disk off after the firing. This spot is also a good place to mark you signature with a black underglaze covered with wax resist if you didn't inscribe it in the clay earlier.

3 Always stir your glaze just before you use it. Check for lumps and check to see if it is the thickness you want, using a hydrometer, if you have one (see Mixing Glazes, page 44), or using a small test piece. Dip two thirds of the plate into the glaze for a few seconds and then lift it out

and allow the drips to stop before you put it down (photo 54). Don't touch the wet glazed surface. When the glaze is dry, carefully hold the glazed side and dip the plate in again, so there is an overlap (photo 55). Allow the plate to drip and dry.

4 With a sponge, clean any glaze off the waxed areas so that when the plate is placed on the kiln shelf, no glazed area touches the shelf (photo 56). Glaze the bowl in the same manner.

5 Glaze the tumbler and pitcher by first pouring glaze into the interiors and pouring it back out, turning the pieces in a smooth even motion so that the rims are evenly covered with glaze (photo 57).

6 To glaze the outside of the tumbler, dip it into the glaze just short of the bottom edge. Here, I've chosen to dip on an angle so that more of the natural clay color will show and some of the monotony of right angles will be alleviated (photo 58).

7 Glaze the outside of the pitcher the same way as the tumbler. If your bucket is not deep enough to dip your pitcher, use a cup to pour the glaze onto it, holding the pitcher upside down over the bucket.

8 Handle the glazed ware carefully when placing it in the

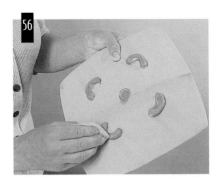

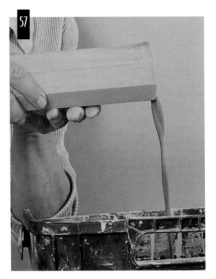

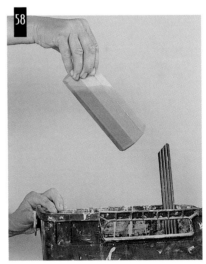

kiln; the raw glaze coating is fragile. Use a small brush to touch up areas where glaze has chipped or rubbed off or where there are pinholes in the glaze coverage.

9 Fire to Δ03.

CHAPTER 3

WINTER RUSTIC SETTING

This place setting requires a bit more preparation than the others, but once you've made the bisqued-clay press molds, the construction of the plates and bowls is a cinch. I like using bisqued-clay for molds because it's quite durable (it doesn't chip like plaster), it lasts forever, and it's porous, so clay can be molded directly onto it without sticking. You can make the molds in any shape you like; feel free to modify the design for round plates I've shown here. If you have access to a potter's wheel, it can help speed up the construction of round molds. So can a lazy Susan turntable, but neither is essential.

I experimented with different glazes that would break nicely over texture, looking for one that would highlight rather than obscure this set's carved border design. The Chameleon glaze I chose is so named because it shows a degree of variation depending on its thickness and the firing schedule and temperature. Once you achieve consistency in terms of application amount and your firing and cooling schedule, you'll be able to eliminate some of the unpredictable results that this glaze can produce. But then again, if you're like me, the unpredictability may be why you end up liking it so much. Nevertheless, I've included a few tips to help you rein in the unknowns a bit. A traditional celadon glaze would also work nicely here. It's often used to great effect over relief areas because it pools in crevices and breaks thinly over raised areas.

Materials and Tools

- ▲ Turntable (optional)
- ▲ Shapes for making the molds, such as plastic disc snow sleds, lighting fixture covers, mixing bowls, pillows, or carved polystyrene foam
- ▲ Plastic sheeting
- ▲ Poster board
- ▲ Protractor (if you're creating circular forms)
- ▲ Ruler
- ▲ Pen or pencil
- ▲ Scissors
- ▲ Approximately 25 lbs. (11.35 kg) of any clay for the molds
- ▲ Cutting wire
- ▲ Rolling pin, wooden dowel, or slab roller

- ▲ Canvas
- ▲ Several ware boards
- ▲ Knife
- ▲ Loop carving tools
- ▲ 25 lbs. (11.35 kg) porcelain clay for Δ5 to Δ6 oxidation firing (per place setting)
- ▲ Rubber or metal rib
- ▲ Pony roller
- ▲ Scoring tool
- ▲ Slip
- ▲ Small brushes
- ▲ Sponge
- ▲ Wood rasp (optional)
- ▲ Stoppers for salt and pepper set
- ▲ Needle tool

- ▲ Wax resist
- ▲ 5 gallons (19 L) Chameleon Glaze (See Appendix D for formula.)
- ▲ Glaze hydrometer
- ▲ Glaze tongs
- ▲ Craft knife (optional)
- ▲ Small amount (approximately 1 tablespoon) of a contrasting glaze (Simply add a stain color of your choice to the Clear Glaze formula in Appendix D.)

Starting Tip

- ▲ Working on a turntable will make creating these round shapes easier.

PRESS MOLD STEPS

1 Choose some rounded forms to use in making the molds. You can use something as basic as a pillow, if nothing else is available, or even a ball of plastic. You can also combine different objects, adding clay here and there to create just the shape you need. Here, I've added clay to the bottom of a mixing bowl to create the shape I wanted for the plate mold (photo 1), then covered the mold with two layers of plastic (photo 2). Be sure to use two layers of plastic over the mold if you have added clay, or you'll find it difficult to remove your slab from the mold later.

2 After choosing the shapes for the plates and bowls, decide how big to make each, taking into account the shrinkage factor in both the clay molds and the final pieces. For example, the molds will probably shrink about five percent during the drying and bisque-firing process, then the final pieces made from those molds will shrink an average of approximately 10 percent. Therefore, the pieces you cut out to make your molds need to be about 15 percent larger than what you want your final plates and bowls to be. My greenware (unfired) plate mold, for instance, was 14 inches (35 cm) in diame-

ter; the finished, fired plate turned out to be 12 inches (30 cm) in diameter.

3 For the set's small, flared coffee cup, test some fan shapes with poster board until you come up with a good shape (the protractor will help here). Don't forget to enlarge it for shrinkage. For both the tripod cup variation and the salt and pepper set, you'll need a rectangular shape measuring approximately 7 x 12 inches (17.5 x 30 cm). (An alternative is to make this rectangular template wider and longer than you think you'll need now, to give you some flexibility later in case you decide to make a wider or taller cup.)

4 From the clay you've chosen for your molds, roll out slabs ¾ inch (1.9 cm) thick, use a protractor to cut out your plate and bowl pieces, and slump the pieces over the forms you chose or created in step 1. You may need to add a coil of clay under the slabs, in some cases, to build them up (photo 3).

5 After the clay molds have dried to leather hard, carve into the outside borders with a loop carving tool to create a design (photo 4). Turning the piece on the turntable, if you're using one, carve a line to delineate the edge of the piece. Remember: the molds you are constructing will form the insides of your plates and bowls, and your finished pieces will be the reverse of the carvings. Before spending a long time on each mold, it's a good idea to create a test carving, fire it, and then press clay onto it to get an idea of how deep the carving needs to be. To ensure a good release of the clay from the mold later, don't create undercuts (negative spaces that leave clay stuck in crevices) (see figure 1). If you spend the extra time it takes to make perfectly shaped and carved molds, you'll reap the benefits later, especially if you plan to use your molds repeatedly, so don't rush through this step.

6 If the rims of the bowl and plate molds are wide, consider sloping them upward slightly. (Rims that are too wide and flat will be prone to warping later in the firing.) On the saucer mold, add to the center a small disc of clay ⅛ inch (3 mm) thick and the diameter of the cup base. The disc will form an indentation (where the cup will rest) in the final piece.

Figure 1

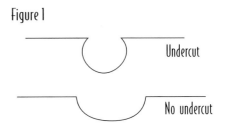

Undercut

No undercut

7 Cut the flat molds for the cups and salt and pepper shakers out of slabs ½ inch (1.3 cm) thick, then carve your design along one border of each. Also, use a carved line to delineate the top edge of the mold, to make it easier later to make a precise edge or lip on the pieces. After the pieces have dried, bisque fire them.

As the finished molds in photo 5 show, an alternative to making separate bowl molds is to make a removable clay dome shape to go over the plate molds (turning them into bowl molds when you need them). This option saves time at the mold-making stage, but may slow you down during production.

PLATE STEPS

1 First, make poster-board templates in sizes to fit your molds. For the dinner plate (working with the porcelain clay), roll out a slab ³⁄₈ inch (9 mm) thick and the size of your plate template. Lift it carefully, trying not to distort it, and lay it on the mold (photo 6). If you find this difficult to do without stretching the slab, with the slab on a large piece of canvas, lay the mold upside down on the slab, fold the canvas over the mold, then flip the whole sandwich over.

2 Use your fingers to press the clay firmly onto the mold, all the way around the border part of the piece (photo 7). Experience will tell you how much pressing it takes to pick up the impression of the carved texture. I liked the pebbly texture that showed where my fingers had pressed, so I left it on my pieces, but you may prefer to smooth it over with a rib, pony roller, or wooden dowel. Trim off the excess clay around the edge of the piece, letting the outside of the mold guide your knife.

3 To make feet, roll out three coils, each 4 inches (10 cm) long and ½ inch (1.3 cm) thick in the middle, tapered on the ends. Curl up the ends and curve the pieces (photo 8). Score the feet and their spots on the bottom of the plate, apply slip, and pinch them onto the scored places (photo 9). Other alternatives include adding a foot rim or adding feet made in other shapes.

4 Rest a ware board on top of the feet to level them (photo 10).

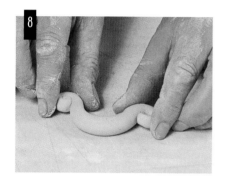

5 Repeat steps 1 through 4 to make the salad plate and the saucer. You may want to use a slab slightly thinner than ¼ inch (6 mm) for the saucer.

6 After adding feet to all the plates, allow the clay to stiffen to leather hard on the molds. Then, place a flat ware board on the feet and flip each plate upright. Remove the mold. Using the carved line that delineates the edge as a guide, trim and smooth the outer edge of each plate with a knife and sponge or a rasp (photo 11).

Tip

A wood rasp is a handy tool for shaving off small amounts of clay to even out an edge, especially if you have waited until the piece is past leather hard.

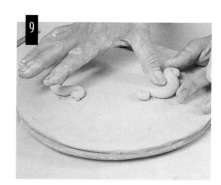

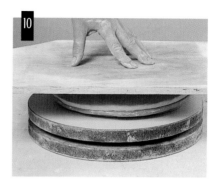

BOWL VARIATION

The only difference between the plates and the bowls is that the diameter of the clay circles you cut for the bowls will need to be ½ to 1 inch (1.3 to 2.5 cm) larger than the diameter of the molds, depending on how deep the bowl mold is. Carefully press the clay onto the molds so that the extra fullness is evenly distributed around the forms. You don't want folds in the clay. And, again, use *two* layers of plastic between the mold and your slab if you have improvised and used clay to adhere a dome mold form onto your plate mold to create a bowl mold.

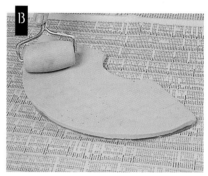

Coffee Cup

1 Roll out a slab ⅛ to 3/16 inch (3 to 5 mm) thick, use a template to cut out the cup's shape, and press the shape onto the carved, fan-shaped mold (photo 12). Save a piece of the slab to use later for the cup bottom.

2 With this piece, it would be a better idea to smooth out the pebbly, finger-pressed texture, since this area will be on the inside of the cup (photo 13).

3 Trim off excess clay from the ends that will be joined to form the cup, cutting them on a bevel. Peel the slab off the mold, and trim the top edge along the raised line (photo 14). Curve the slab, and allow it to rest upside down in this cone shape until it stiffens and is almost leather hard.

4 Score the edges, apply slip, and overlap one edge just a little as you join them (photo 15).

5 Score a circle on the leftover slab to correspond to the cup base, score the cup base, apply slip, and join these two pieces, trimming off the excess clay and smoothing the edges (photo 16). Press a slight indentation into the bottom of the cup so that it won't rock.

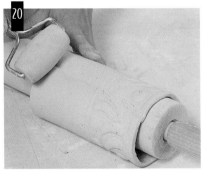

6 I chose a coil handle for the cup, to match the coiled feet on the other pieces, but there are numerous ways to make handles. See pages 102 and 103 for other options. By rolling up the bottom part of the coiled handle, you create an area that keeps the coffee drinker's finger from resting on the hot cup (photo 17). Press the handle onto the scored areas on the seam of the cup (photo 18). Allow the cup to dry slowly, watching to make sure the handle doesn't dry completely before the cup is dry.

Tripod Cup

1 Roll out a slab ⅛ to ³⁄₁₆ inch (3 to 5 mm) thick and measuring approximately 6 x 9 inches (15 x 22.5 cm), press it onto the rectangular mold, then smooth out the pebbly, finger-pressed texture (photo 19).

2 Join the edges of the slab around a rolling pin, and seal the seam by pressing it gently or by rolling over the seam with a pony roller or a wooden dowel (photo 20).

3 Position the joined rectangle upside down. Score the bottom edges, and fold them in to form three legs (photo 21).

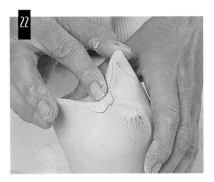

4 Smooth the seams of the legs on both the inside and outside. You may have to add a little button of clay to fill in the center (photo 22). You may also want to add a little clay inside the tips of the legs, so the cup is not too hard to clean later (photo 23). Add a coil handle (see Coffee Cup, step 6). Let the cup dry slowly.

SALT & PEPPER SHAKER STEPS

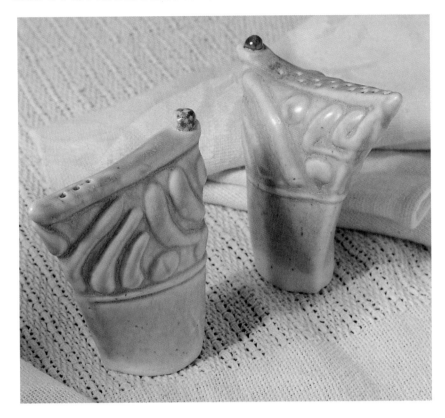

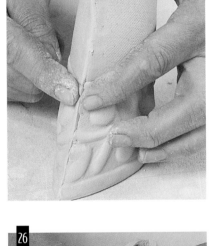

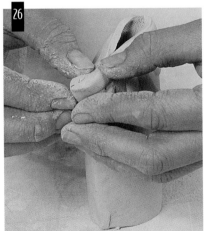

It's a good idea to have the stoppers that you want to use for your salt and pepper shakers before you start on these pieces, so you can make the indented holes in the bottom of the shakers just the right size. Small corks will work, but many ceramic suppliers stock little rubber stoppers in a variety of sizes. It's very difficult, once the pieces are fired, to drill holes for these stoppers or make your holes bigger. Therefore, you may decide it's worthwhile to fire a test piece to make sure you've calculated the shrinkage correctly.

1 Press a slab ³⁄₁₆ inch (5 mm) thick and measuring approximately 7 inches (17.5 cm) long and 4 inches (10 cm) wide into the rectangular mold. Bevel the side edges as you cut out a wedge shape (see photo 24).

2 Curve the wedge around to form a slightly flattened tube. Fold in the top edges, and allow this shape to stiffen slightly before scoring the seams, applying slip, and joining first the side seam and then the top (photos 25 and 26).

3 Score a circle on the leftover slab to correspond to the base of the shaker, score the base, apply slip, and join the two pieces, trimming off the excess clay (photo 27) and smoothing the edges.

4 After the piece has stiffened somewhat, cut out a hole in the bottom for the stopper (photo 28), and indent the area slightly with a wet finger (photo 29).

5 Use the needle tool to make the holes in the top of the piece (photo 30). You may need to experiment to get these just the right size, since the final size of the holes will also be affected by the glazing.

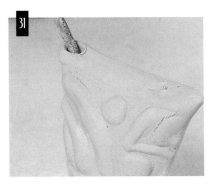

6 Add a small piece of adornment if you don't want the piece to look quite so plain. Here, I'm making a small indentation in the top (photo 31), where I'll rest a separate little ball of clay. During glazing, I'll glaze the ball with a contrasting color and allow the glaze to fuse the ball onto the piece. It's all merely to add a dot of color that, for me, enlivens the work and gives it a bit of sparkle. Repeat steps 1 through 6 to make your second shaker.

GLAZING STEPS

1 After bisque firing the pieces, wax the areas of any pieces that will touch the kiln shelves or come within ¼ inch (6 mm) of the shelves. Allow the wax to dry before glazing the pieces.

2 You'll dip each piece into the Chameleon glaze, attempting to cover the whole surface of the piece with one dip, so make sure you have an adequate amount of glaze mixed. Always stir the glaze well before using it. Though I don't always adjust the thickness of all my glazes in a precise manner, this is one glaze that benefits from a close monitoring of thickness by using a hydrometer (photo 32). See page 44 in Chapter 1 for details on using a hydrometer. If your glaze is too thick, it will be charcoal gray; if it's too thin, it will be a pale tan-green. When it is just right, it will be a textured green with gray crystals in the recesses. A few test firings first will help you determine the right thickness. Chameleon is not a particularly runny glaze unless it is both too thick and overfired.

3 Using the glaze tongs to hold the plates and bowls, dip each piece completely in the glaze, then allow it to drip (photo 33) and finally to dry. Use a brush to touch up any spots, if necessary, and to glaze the places where the tongs made a mark.

Tip

You can use a sharp knife (a craft knife is perfect) to shave off thickened areas on the glaze, such as drips.

4 Glaze the cups by first pouring the glaze into the interiors and then slowly pouring it out, coating the entire insides and rims as you pour. Try to accomplish this in one pour, so you don't have to add more glaze to finish, which would thicken the glaze coating in some areas.

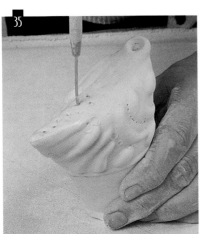

5 Glaze the salt and pepper set by holding the bases and dipping each piece upside down, allowing the glaze to reach up to ¼ inch (6 mm) from the bottom (photo 34).

6 Check the holes in the top of the shakers to make sure they are not clogged with glaze. Use the needle tool if you need to clean them (photo 35). With a sponge, clean off any glaze remaining on the bottom rims of the shakers.

7 Glaze the tiny balls that decorate the salt and pepper shakers in a contrasting color, if you like. Set them in place, and the glaze will fuse them to the shaker during the firing process (photo 36).

8 Fire the pieces to Δ5. See Appendix D for special instructions on firing this particular glaze. Lengthening the cooling cycle produces a more interesting surface. If the glaze has been applied too thickly and as a result turns out too dark, try refiring it to a slightly higher temperature.

> We always eat first
> with our eyes.
> Presentation is
> as important
> as preparation.
>
> Mark Rosenstein
> Chef
> Continental cuisine

CHAPTER 4

SPRING TEA SETTING

This is the place setting to make when you have some great Asian food to serve. (A little sushi perhaps? The cone-shaped bowl is just right for getting those last grains of rice picked up with chopsticks.) But the setting works just as well for sandwiches and soup. The overlapping layers of clay that form the seams are not smoothed over, and the rims are left uneven to emphasize the natural similarities between soft clay slabs and fabric. For this reason, cutting, folding, and shaping paper is a good way to work out the shapes and sizes you want to use for the cup, bowl, and teapot.

The plates (rectangular or whatever shape you choose) are formed over a mold that you make out of wood or sheetrock. The corners are shaped to construct a standing rim, and the plates may or may not have some feet attached. The teapot, with the same cone geometry as the bowl and cup, may be a more challenging object to make, but it's also one that offers lots of room for your creativity to run wild.

Though any fine-textured clay would work for this project, I've chosen a mid-range $\Delta 5$ porcelain. The glaze is a clear base with the addition of ceramic stains to make two different colors that will show up brightly over the pure white clay. I chose black for one of the colors because I like the dramatic way food looks on a black backdrop. Commercial ceramic stains come in an enormous range of colors, so you could concoct any number of color combinations. Serious tea drinkers often want cups with white interiors, so they can appreciate the subtle shades of the brew. If you fall into this category, just use the base glaze with no stain additions on the inside of the cups. You'll dip your pieces in both glaze colors, with the colors overlapping on the plates.

Materials and Tools

- ▲ Cardboard
- ▲ Scissors
- ▲ Pen or pencil
- ▲ Ruler
- ▲ Pieces of sheetrock, wood, or plywood for plate molds (If you're using wood, you'll also need a jigsaw and sandpaper.)
- ▲ Knife
- ▲ Wood screws and screwdriver or construction adhesive (if you want to make your molds of multiple layers)
- ▲ Sheetrock spackling compound (optional)
- ▲ Wood rasp (optional)
- ▲ Approximately 25 lbs. (11.35 kg) porcelain clay for Δ5 oxidation firing (per place setting)
- ▲ Cutting wire

- ▲ Rolling pin, wooden dowel, or slab roller
- ▲ Canvas
- ▲ Several ware boards
- ▲ Thin fabric, such as muslin, to cover the molds
- ▲ Stick of wood (1 x 2 x 12 inches [2.5 x 5 x 30 cm])
- ▲ Wooden paddle
- ▲ Sponge
- ▲ Scoring tool
- ▲ Slip
- ▲ Several small brushes
- ▲ Tape
- ▲ Small wooden dowel
- ▲ Assorted texturizing tools (optional)
- ▲ Shallow bowl
- ▲ Cookie cutters or other cutting tools in various shapes (optional)

- ▲ Needle tool
- ▲ Piece of plastic wrap
- ▲ Hole tool (⅛ inch [3 mm])
- ▲ Air compressor (optional)
- ▲ Wax resist
- ▲ 4000 grams of clear glaze with black stain added and 2000 grams of clear glaze with aqua stain added (See Appendix D for formulas.)
- ▲ Glaze tongs (optional)
- ▲ Piece of wire

Starting Tip

- ▲ Cutting, folding, and shaping paper or thin cardboard is one of the best ways to experiment with shapes and sizes for your cups, bowls, and teapot. Have some on hand to work with.

PLATE STEPS

1 Decide on the shape and sizes of your plates. Then, considering shrinkage, decide what sizes your molds need to be to create soft greenware pieces that have the interior dimensions and rim depth you want. Shrinkage is often higher with a porcelain clay body than with other clays. (See page 13 for details on calculating shrinkage.) To get your molds thick enough to make your plate rims, you may need to put two layers of mold material together. The rims on the plates in the set I made are approximately 1 inch (2.5 cm) high; I glued together two pieces of ½-inch (1.3 cm) sheetrock to create them.

2 Cut your mold shapes out of boards, plywood, or sheetrock. Your molds should measure what you want the *interior dimensions* of your greenware (unfired) plates to be. I made plate molds that measured approximately 7 x 9¾ inches (17.5 x 24.7 cm) and 9½ x 12½ inches (23.8 x 31.3 cm). The *outside dimensions* of my final plates from those molds measured 6¾ x 9½ inches (17.1 x 23.8 cm) and 9⅛ x 12 inches (23.1 x 30 cm).

3 After making your molds, round off the edges, and make sure there is some flare from the base of the molds to the rim. In other words, avoid any undercuts on your molds, so it won't be difficult to remove clay from them. (Figure 1 on page 67 illustrates

the difference between a piece with an undercut and one without.) I chose to make my molds from sheetrock, because this material is easy to cut by scoring, snapping, and then slicing with a sharp knife. I screwed the two layers together, but you could also glue them with any construction adhesive, such as silicone. If you're working with sheetrock, it's good to have a little sheetrock spackling compound on hand in case you find imperfections you want to fill in. You can then use a wood rasp to easily shape the edges of the sheetrock. If you use a jigsaw and wood, make your cuts with a slight angle, again so you create a mold from which you can easily remove your clay.

4 For each plate size, make a cardboard template, allowing for the extra amount of clay you'll need to create the rim of the plate. Roll out a slab ¼ inch (6 mm) thick and a few inches (cm) bigger than your mold. Using your cardboard template, cut out the plate shape (photo 1), saving the leftover edges of the slab for the plate's feet.

5 Place a piece of fabric over the mold, and drape the clay slab over the fabric. Or, if you're worried about distorting the clay slab as you drape it, with the slab on a piece of canvas or a ware board, place the fabric over the slab, then place the mold on top, and

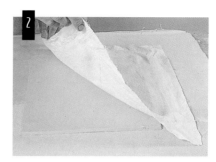

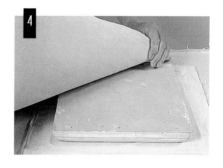

cover the mold with canvas (photos 2 through 4). You can then turn the whole sandwich over. This approach makes the clay less prone to warpage.

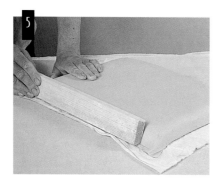

6 Form the corners of the plate by paddling them to compress and conform the clay to the shape of the mold (photo 5). You could also slice the four corners with a knife, score the flaps you create by doing so, apply slip to the flaps, and fold one over the other at each corner.

7 Trim the edge of the plate to make it level (photo 6). Allow the plate and the piece of slab you're saving for the feet to dry at the same rate. Keep a careful eye on the drying here. If the plate dries too much while it's on the mold, it will crack as it shrinks.

8 From the leftover slab piece, cut out shapes to use as feet for the plate (photo 7). These can be any shape or size—or you can choose not to have feet at all. I chose to add feet because they make the plates more elegant and because, with feet, more of the underside of the plates can be glazed. The feet will, of course, make the plates heavier.

9 Attach the feet to the plate bottom by scoring the feet and the spots where they'll go, applying slip, and pressing them in place (photo 8).

Tip

If the plate refuses to stay flat in the glaze firing, insisting on sagging in certain areas, you can adjust the size and placement of the plate's feet to strengthen weak areas.

10 Separate the plate from the mold by placing a clean, flat board on top of the plate and flipping it over. Remove the mold, then the fabric. Check the corners to make sure there are no deep creases that need to be filled in with clay. Smooth and even out the rim, if necessary (photo 9), and allow the plate to dry slowly and evenly.

CUP AND BOWL STEPS

1 Roll out a thinner slab, one about ⅛ inch (3 mm) thick, for the cup and the bowl.

2 Experiment with hemispherical cardboard templates for each. Fold and tape your templates in different ways, and play with different heights and widths. The template radius for my cup measured 4 inches (10 cm), and the template radius for my bowl measured 6 inches (15 cm). You may find that the bowl template needs to extend beyond a true hemisphere shape (to make it more open) and that the cup template needs to be slightly less than a true hemisphere. In order to emphasize the overlapping seams, I made the rims of my pieces uneven by widening one end of the shape used to create each, but you could just as easily make the rims even. When making your decision about the rims, you may want to consider whether the pieces will eventually be stored upright or upside down.

3 Use your template to cut out a shape for the cup (photo 10).

4 Gently curve the shape into a cone with overlapping seams (photo 11). You may find this is easier if you hold the form upside down as you work. If your cone just folds up and collapses, let the clay stiffen a bit more, but not too much, or it may develop a crack later. Remember that a thin slab will dry faster than a thick one. Allow the clay to stiffen somewhat in the cone form before you make the seam. The less you handle the piece at its softer stage, the less you'll disturb the fresh, crisp look of the slab.

Tip

When forming a curved piece, bend it around a little farther than it needs to go, and allow it to stiffen somewhat in this exaggerated form. Clay has a tendency to want to return to its original shape, so this helps compensate for the curve's propensity to flatten.

5 While the cone dries, make the base of the piece. Roll out a long coil (about 20 inches [50 cm] long if you're working on the bowl, 16 inches [40 cm] long if you're working on the cup, and approximately ¼ inch [6 mm]

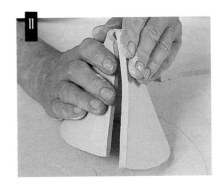

thick). Taper the ends, and twist the coil of clay into a round dome, leaving a hole in the middle (photo 12).

6 Smooth and pinch the coils together on the underside (photo 13). Again, to preserve the texture, allow the dome to dry a little before handling it.

7 Go back to the cone, which has stiffened somewhat. Score the area where the edges overlap, apply slip (photo 14), and press the edges together, overlapping them about ½ inch (1.3 cm).

8 Using a small wooden dowel or your finger, firm this seam from the inside, with the cone lying on its side (photo 15). With a sponge, wipe away any slip that squishes out, and smooth the seam's edges and the upper rim without obliterating the seam or the geometry of the crisp edges.

9 Press a pea-sized ball of clay into the tip end of the base of the cup to make the finished object easier to clean (photo 16).

10 Score the inside edge of the base coil (the hole area) and the bottom of the cone, and apply slip. Press the two pieces together (photo 17). To my eye it looks great to have a very narrow juncture here, but beware—an extremely narrow juncture may be an invitation to disaster. If it's too

narrow, the weight of the top of the cup or bowl may make it tilt over. Strengthen the join with a coil of clay if it appears to need it. Allow the piece to dry slowly and evenly.

11 For the cup handle, roll out a small slab approximately ¼ inch (6 mm) thick, and allow it to stiffen to the same degree as the cup. Texturize the slab if you like, then try cutting out various handle shapes (photo 18) and holding them up to the cup to visually test them. Consider whether this will be an every-morning cup, cradled in half-asleep hands, or an occasional-use party cup, meant to dazzle and amaze. Imagine how the balance of the handle will feel with a full cup of tea. Do you need to accommodate more than one finger? I chose to cut my handle in a geometric shape, because it seemed to fit with the geometry of the cone, but a contrasting shape could be fun, too.

12 After smoothing the edges of the handle shape, score the handle and the cup where the two pieces will attach, apply slip, and press the pieces firmly together, trying not to distort the cup (photo 19). Add a few buttons of clay to the join to strengthen it and provide a little textural interest. Let the piece dry slowly.

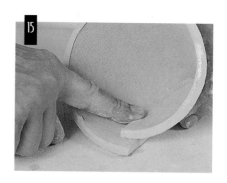

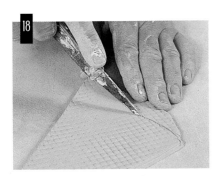

TEAPOT STEPS

Like many potters, I love making teapots. Why? Because it is so challenging to wrestle with the design relationships among handle, lid, knob, spout, body, and foot, attempting to make them all work together on both an aesthetic and a functional level.

The handle, just as on a pitcher, must be strong enough to lift the weight of the pot when it's full— and it should visually convince pourers of its strength. It should also be balanced and comfortable, protecting fingers from having to rest on the hot teapot body and accommodating a full grip if the pot size is going to warrant one. You may need to add a loop or knob in addition to the handle if the pot is particularly large. Other handle options include bamboo handles, available from ceramics suppliers, or handles you make

out of other non-clay materials. A harmonious size relationship between handle and pot may be more difficult to achieve on very small teapots, but it's certainly possible. Consider the little hand-built red clay Yixing teapots made for thousands of years in China. They're well-proportioned and, though small, quite functional. The one below is based on these traditional pots.

Peter Pinnell, *Teapot*, 5" × 8" × 4" (12.7 × 20.3 × 10.2 cm), 1997. Earthenware, slab body and spout, carved handle; slip trailed, terra sigillata, patina finish; Δ04. Photo by artist

Tip

If the cup warps in the firing process, the handle may be too heavy. Either thicken the slab from which you cut the cup or thin the handle slab to lighten it. You might also position the handle closer to the base of the cup, or try propping the cup at an angle (tilted away from the handle side, so the weight of the handle doesn't pull down on the cup) for drying and firing.

The lid should be designed to complement the form of the teapot. It also needs to be large enough to allow easy cleaning of the pot's interior, and it must fit well (so it doesn't fall off during pouring), which means that it is best to make it at the same time you make the pot. If you decide to add a knob to your lid, it should be easy to grip.

Entire chapters in ceramics books have been written on pouring and the dripless spout. There are many factors in spout design that contribute to a nice, smooth, non-dribbling pour. The spout's gully should allow enough liquid to flow smoothly, through adequate strainer holes, and then constrict the flow as the liquid rolls over the spout's lip. You need a thin, sharp (but not too fragile), non-flaring lip to instantly cut the flow of liquid and allow it to drain back down the inside of the spout. The level at which the spout lip is cut off should be at least as high as the full-liquid level of the body of the pot. Within all these rules, you've still got room for endless variations. And remember, even with close attention to every design criteria, you never know exactly how the pot will pour until your first cup of tea.

Finally, the foot of your pot should provide stability yet not add too much additional weight. Small feet added to a flat-bottomed pot

may give it just enough lift to keep it from appearing clunky. You also have the option of making a special stand to display the teapot when it is not being used.

Teapots are time-consuming, but the challenges and the opportunities for creating pots with distinct personalities continue to fascinate potters. With a project that has so many parts, you may want to start by making all the parts first and letting them stiffen together, paying special attention that the smaller ones don't dry out more than the larger ones. In the steps that follow, however, I demonstrate making the parts as I go.

1 Begin with a slab about $^3/_{16}$ to $^1/_4$ inch (5 to 6 mm) thick, and measuring approximately 20 x 20 inches (50 x 50 cm). In addition, roll out a thicker slab for the handle, $^1/_4$ inch (6 mm) or more in thickness and measuring approximately 10 x 10 inches (25 x 25 cm). (This handle slab is bigger than you'll need, but it's always good to have some extra stiff clay handy in case you want to try out several different handle options.)

2 Create a cardboard template for the teapot body, similar to the ones you used for the cup and the bowl. (I used a hemisphere template with a radius of 10 inches [25 cm]). The rim of the teapot body should be even. Once the larger slab is somewhat stiff, use

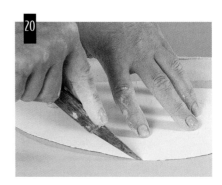

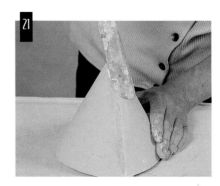

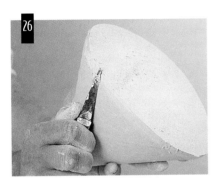

the template to cut out the shape for the teapot body (photo 20).

3 To form the shape into the teapot body, follow the same process you used to create the cup and the bowl. Gently curve the shape into a cone with overlapping seams. You may find this is easier if you hold the form upside down as you work. Allow the clay to stiffen somewhat in the cone form before you make the seam. Once it's stiff, score the area where the edges overlap, apply slip, and press the edges together, overlapping them about ½ inch (1.3 cm); remember that you want the rim to be even on this piece. Paddle the seam to smooth the join (photo 21), and, using the wooden dowel or your finger, firm this seam from the inside, with the cone lying on its side. With a sponge, wipe away any slip that squishes out, and smooth the seam's edges and the upper rim without obliterating the seam or the geometry of the crisp edges. Press a pea-sized ball of clay into the tip end of the base of the pot to make the finished object easier to clean.

4 Cut out a circle about 1 inch (2.5 cm) in diameter larger than the top diameter of the cone (photo 22).

5 Form the circle into a slight dome by using a wad of paper or plastic or a bowl under it and then paddling and shaping it (photo 23). I encourage a domed top here because it is stronger than a flat one. Flat tops will often sag in the firing.

6 Rest the domed circle in a shallow bowl, score around the edge and around the top edge of the cone, and apply slip (photo 24). Press the cone firmly onto the circle, and cut off any excess clay around the edge (photo 25). Paddle the join, and smooth it with a knife (photo 26).

8 Roll out a ⅜-inch (9 mm) thick coil with tapering ends, about 24 inches (60 cm) long, and twist the coil into a round dome, leaving a hole in the middle. Smooth and pinch the coils together on the underside, score the inside edge of the base coil (the hole area) and the bottom of the cone, and apply slip. Press the two pieces together (photo 27). This is a critical area, so make sure it is strong. You may want to add an additional coil to strengthen the join (photo 28).

9 Scribe a circle (or another shape if you prefer) on the domed top of the teapot, and cut the shape out with a sharp knife, or use a cookie cutter, as I have here (photo 29). This job is more neatly accomplished if the clay is leather hard rather than a bit soft. Smooth the edges of the cutout area. If the opening is large

enough, reach inside to smooth the inside of the join between the domed top and the body, and add a coil if possible.

10 Cut out a larger circle (or another shape) than the hole in the top to make the lid (photo 30).

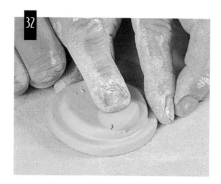

11 Attach the circle you cut out of the top of the pot to the bottom of the lid, scoring the two pieces and applying slip to attach them (photo 31). Next, add a small button of clay to the smaller circle, to act as a stop to keep the lid from falling out when you're pouring liquid from the pot (photo 32).

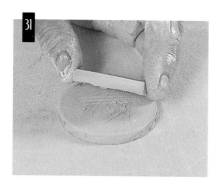

12 Create a knob for the top of the lid. Get out your texturizing tools and try out different textures on different shapes. If the knob turns out to be over ½ inch (1.3 cm) thick, poke a hole in it (through the bottom of the lid) with a needle tool. The hole will help reduce the risk of the knob blowing up in the kiln if you happen to fire it too fast. I have created a slab knob that will rest on two buttons of clay (photo 33). This is only one way to make a lid; there are numerous others. Figure 2 shows some variations.

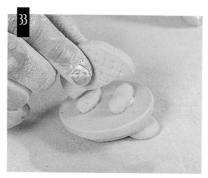

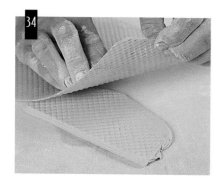

Figure 2: Three variations for lids

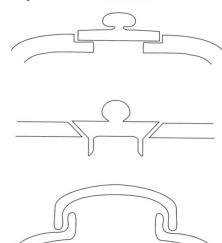

13 Tear off a small piece of thin plastic, push a hole through the middle the size of the opening in the teapot, place it over the opening, and then place the lid on the pot to make sure it fits nicely. You want the fit to be neither too snug nor too loose. The plastic helps keep the lid from sticking to the pot, so you don't have to tug on the knob, which may not be strong enough to withstand tugging before it's fired. At this time, consider whether you will fire the lid on or off the pot. Many potters prefer to fire their lids on their pots, to ensure a good fit (since that way both pieces warp together). In addition, think about where the glaze edge will be around the lid. You may want to incise a line at the edge to make the glazing neater.

14 Roll out a thin slab, about ⅛ inch (3 mm) thick and approximately 10 x 10 inches (25 x 25 cm) for the teapot spout. If you like, texturize all or part of the slab with one of your texturizing tools (photo 34).

15 Cut out a wedge shape (photo 35), and gently roll it around a small wooden dowel to form a cylinder, tapered at one end. Score the edges and apply slip to join them. I suggest making several spouts in different sizes. That way you can choose the one you like best, and you've got several backups if one cracks when you bend it.

16 Decide where you'll join the spout to the pot, and use a hole tool to make small, ⅛-inch (3 mm) strainer holes in that area of the teapot body (photo 36). For a good pour, the area of the holes should exceed the area of the opening of the spout. Always make a few extra holes, too, in case some get clogged with glaze.

17 Give the spout cylinder a bit of a curve, if you like. Flare out the wide end, so you'll have a greater area to attach. Score the wide end and the place on the pot where it will go, apply slip, and attach the spout firmly, being careful not to block the strainer holes

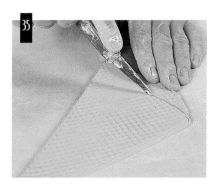

(photo 37). Roll a small coil of clay around the join, if you like.

18 When the end of the spout is leather hard, use a sharp knife to trim it off at an angle level with the top of the pot. Then, use a wet finger or tool to thin and extend the bottom edge to form an extended lip that continues the line of the spout (photo 38). The lip shouldn't droop too far downward, or it will cause liquid to dribble when it's poured. An edge that is too thick or rounded will also cause dribbling. Squeezing the end into an oval shape, so there is a gully for the liquid to funnel through, will also encourage a good pour.

19 To make a handle for your pot, follow the same procedure you used to make the cup handle (step 11, page 82). Cut out several handles from the ¼-inch (6 mm) thick slab, and hold them up to the pot to test them visually for weight and balance. After smoothing the edges of the handle shape, score the handle and the pot where the two pieces will attach, apply slip, and press the pieces firmly together. Allow the pot to dry slowly. When you move it, do so with great care. All the parts are fragile when they are bone dry.

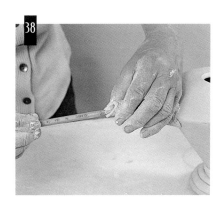

The appropriate size, shape,

and color of each dish

must be effective in enhancing

the food arrangement.

A medium-size round rice bowl,

for example,

is at the center of the

Japanese meal.

Fish and meat are served

on rectangular plates

for better viewing

of their size and shape.

Even the importance

of drinking green tea

from a handmade tea cup

adds to the atmosphere

and uniqueness

of each meal.

Peter Wada
Chef
Asian cuisine

GLAZING STEPS

1 After bisque firing your pieces, brush off any dust and check the interiors for any small pieces of debris. Use a clean brush or compressed air, if you have a compressor.

2 With a brush, apply wax resist to the feet of the plates (or the bottoms of the plates, if you chose not to add feet) and to the bottom edges of the cup, bowl, teapot, and teapot lid. If you are not familiar with the glaze you are using, leave at least a ¼-inch (6 mm) margin between the glaze edge on each piece and the kiln shelf. Allow the resist to dry.

3 After mixing your glazes, stir them, check for lumps, adjust them for thickness, and make sure you have enough glaze to dip your largest object. For the plates, dip three-quarters of each plate into one of the glazes, allow the excess glaze to drip back into the glaze bucket, and then let it dry (photo 39).

4 Dip a quarter of the other end of each plate into the other glaze, overlapping the two colors about ½ inch (1.3 cm). Hold the plates carefully; the glaze coating is fragile at this point. After the glaze dries, sponge off any that adhered to the waxed areas.

5 Glaze the insides of the containers by pouring glaze into the interiors and pouring it back out, turning the pieces in smooth, even motions so that the rims are covered (photo 40). It takes some practice to get the hang of pouring in such a way that you cover the entire interior with one smooth pour.

6 Make sure the strainer holes and the spout on the teapot are not clogged with glaze. Use a piece of wire to unplug them, if necessary. Some potters wax a circle where the holes are before glazing, to prevent clogging. I prefer to adjust the glaze so it's a little thinner for the insides of teapots. You can use a sharp knife to pare down the glaze on the tip of the spout, if there is too much accumulation there (remember that you don't want too round an edge there). But don't scrape off all the glaze.

7 Glaze the outside of the containers by dipping the top parts into the glaze you used on the inside, up to the juncture between the cone and the base (photo 41). Allow them to drip dry. Then, turn the pieces over and dip the bases into the other glaze, overlapping the two glazes a fraction (photo 42). Glaze the lid in the same manner or use glaze tongs to dip it in the glaze. Wipe off any glaze remaining on waxed areas.

8 If you have decided to fire the lid on the teapot, wax the areas that will be touching each other, and leave a margin between the glazes in case either glaze flows in the firing process. Nothing is more frustrating than a lid stuck firmly with glaze onto a fired pot. (Sometimes when this happens, however, it will only appear to be stuck. A sharp rap with a wooden stick can loosen it when the pot is removed from the kiln.)

9 You may want to glaze your lid and knob differently, as I have here (photo 43). The glaze will fuse the knob to the clay buttons on top of the lid when it's fired.

Tip

Add a teaspoon of alumina hydrate to 1 cup (.24 L) of wax resist, and use this where two areas are touching and you don't want glaze (such as where a lid fits on a pot). The wax will burn off and leave the powdery alumina separating the adjoining clay areas. You can brush off the alumina after the firing. Keep this mixture clearly marked. You never want to accidentally use it in place of pure wax resist when you are waxing on top of an underglaze decoration or on top of a glaze; it will make the area rough after the firing.

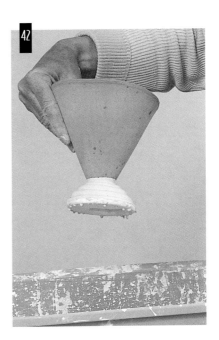

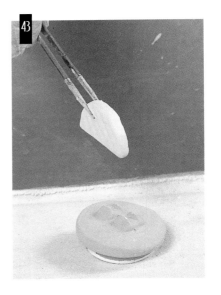

10 Before the pieces are loaded into the kiln, use a small brush to touch up any areas missed by the glaze or to repair places where the glaze has chipped or rubbed off. Handle the pieces carefully; the raw glaze coating is fragile.

11 Fire to Δ5.

CHAPTER 5

SUMMER'S BOUNTY SETTING

I first arrived at the idea of slumping clay into a void in a mold when I was experimenting with melting glass in my kiln. I was heating the glass enough to allow it to bubble out of the openings in some clay wall sconces, and I loved the resulting shapes of the bubbled glass. I then realized that a soft clay slab could stretch enough to form a beautiful curve, too, if I allowed gravity to aid in the forming process.

The key word to remember here is *allow*. It will be tempting to push the clay into the hole in your mold, but the prettiest, smoothest curves will be the ones you don't touch or push. Simply lay a slab of clay over the hole (with a thin piece of fabric between the clay and the mold) and allow it to slump gradually, coaxing it by tapping the edges of the mold to cause the clay to stretch. Allowing the clay to droop on its own, with the fabric helping it to glide smoothly and preventing it from sticking, will result in soft, fluid, elegant curves. Then, the cut rims of your pieces will contrast with and highlight those curves. The shapes and sizes of both the inside slumped area and the outside rim can vary widely. The only inside shape I've found that doesn't work well for the slumped area is one with a protruding sharp angle, which will cause the clay to stretch too thinly. The clay will then tend to tear when it's slumped, or perhaps crack later.

This setting would be elegant simply glazed with a clear glaze over a white clay, but I chose to jazz it up with colorful brush strokes of underglazes, then sprayed a clear glaze on top. If you don't have spray equipment, you can just as easily dip the pieces in the clear glaze, using tongs to hold them.

Materials and Tools

- ▲ Thin pieces of sheetrock or plywood, ½ to 1 inch (1.3 to 2.5 cm) thick and 1 to 3 feet (30 to 90 cm) square, and wooden slats ¼ to 2 inches (6 mm to 5 cm) thick and 1 to 3 feet (30 to 90 cm) long
- ▲ Small amount of spackling compound if you use sheetrock
- ▲ Saber saw
- ▲ Drill (for starting your saw blade) with drill bit diameter to accommodate the size of the saw blade
- ▲ Wood screws or construction adhesive to fasten wooden slats to mold boards (optional)
- ▲ Wood rasp
- ▲ Sandpaper
- ▲ Canvas
- ▲ Several ware boards
- ▲ Approximately 25 lbs. (11.35 kg) white clay for Δ3 to Δ6 oxidation firing (per place setting)
- ▲ Cutting wire

- ▲ Rolling pin, wooden dowel, or slab roller
- ▲ Thin, stretchy fabric, such as muslin
- ▲ Pony roller (optional)
- ▲ Cardboard
- ▲ Pen or pencil
- ▲ Ruler
- ▲ Scissors
- ▲ Toothpick
- ▲ Knife
- ▲ Scoring tool
- ▲ Slip
- ▲ Several small brushes
- ▲ Sponge
- ▲ Wooden paddle
- ▲ Needle tool or other interesting tool for inscribing lines
- ▲ Pieces of plastic wrap such as drycleaning bags
- ▲ Various texturizing tools
- ▲ Cardboard mailing tube or wooden dowel
- ▲ Newspaper

- ▲ String
- ▲ Long-handled stiff brush
- ▲ Wax resist
- ▲ Underglazes (optional) (You can either buy commercial underglazes or add stains of your choice to the underglaze formula in Appendix D.)
- ▲ Clear glaze (See Appendix D for formula.) (1 gallon [3.8 L] for spraying or 5 gallons [19 L] for dipping)
- ▲ Spray booth, respirator, spray gun, and air compressor (if you're spraying the glaze)
- ▲ Glaze tongs and bucket (if you're dipping your pieces to glaze)

Starting Tips

- ▲ Though slumping clay in a mold looks quite effortless, there are a couple of tricks to keep in mind if you want the rims to resist warping and slumping when you fire them. I'll let you in on them when we go through the steps of shaping the rims.

PLATE AND BOWL MOLD STEPS

The molds for this project are simply flat pieces of any material in which you can cut a hole with a knife or saw. I worked with sheetrock and plywood (photo 1). For the smaller, flatter items, the sheetrock worked fine and was easy to cut and shape. However, the larger, deeper pieces required more tapping to slump the clay, so plywood held up better for these and was worth the small amount of extra effort

required to cut and shape it. Masonite, formica, Plexiglas, foam core, and heavy cardboard could also work as mold materials, depending on the size of the mold you're making. (With some less-sturdy mold materials, you might want to add reinforcing wooden sticks to the underside of the mold pieces.)

1 For the large plate mold, cut a hole 10 inches (25 cm) in diameter out of a flat piece of mold material measuring 16 x 16 inches (40 x 40 cm). Use a saw blade set at a 45° angle to make the cut. This angled cut will allow the clay to flow more smoothly over the edge (a sharp angle would weaken the clay in that area). The plywood I'm using here is ½ inch (1.3 cm) thick, the same amount I want the clay to slump in the mold, so I don't have to make any adjustments. If you're working with a thinner material or you want your clay to slump more deeply, use wood screws or construction adhesive to add wooden slats to the bottom of the mold to raise the board off your worktable. Or, you can just rest the mold board on the wooden slats. Next, smooth the inner edge of the mold with the rasp and sandpaper (photo 2).

2 For the bowl and the medium-size plate molds, cut holes 8 inches (20 cm) in diameter out of

pieces of mold material, each measuring 15 x 15 inches (37.5 x 37.5 cm). Decide how deep you want to make the bowl, and use wood screws or construction adhesive to add the appropriate thickness of wooden sticks to the bottom of one mold. (You may want to try making a piece first before you attach the wooden supports.) Or, if you want to use the same mold for both the bowl and the small plate, just use the sticks (or any support) to rest the mold on while slumping the clay for the bowl.

3 For the small plate, cut a hole 6 inches (15 cm) in diameter out of a piece of mold material measuring 13 x 13 inches (32.5 x 32.5 cm). The mold for the platter needs an irregularly shaped opening measuring 11 inches (27.5 cm) wide and 17 inches (42.5 cm) long. Cut the platter mold out of a piece of mold material measuring 20 x 25 inches (50 x 63.5 cm).

The components of dining are:

a well-set table,

food prepared with love,

a great bottle of wine,

a kindred soul or souls

to share with.

Victor Giancola
Chef
Italian cuisine

PLATE, BOWL, AND PLATTER STEPS

1 Begin with the larger plate. On a piece of canvas, roll out a slab measuring approximately 15 x 15 inches (37.5 x 37.5 cm) and $^3/_8$ inch (9 mm) thick. Place a thin piece of fabric over the slab. Lay the large plate mold on top of the fabric, with the larger diameter side of the beveled opening facing down toward the fabric (photo 3), then flip the entire sandwich over. Why not just pick up the slab and lay it on top of the mold? I've found that handling the slab can distort it slightly, which can cause the plate to warp later.

2 Tap the edges of the mold on the table to allow the clay to slump slightly through the opening. You want it to slump just enough so that when the mold sits on the table, the bottom of the plate touches the table and flattens out a small amount (photo 4).

3 With the rolling pin, wooden dowel, or pony roller, *very* gently flatten the rim of the plate to emphasize the change in direction in the angle of the clay (photo 5), but don't roll too much! This is an area where the slab has already thinned, so it will be

weaker. The rim will be prone to warping downward later if it is further thinned. For a gentler, more rounded curve, don't flatten the rim at all.

4 Decide what shape you want the rim of your plate to be. I chose a modified triangle shape in order to contrast with the circular opening. Cut a template out of cardboard if you want to reproduce the same shape on another plate. Otherwise, you may want to cut each rim a little differently. You can cut any number of unusual shapes. Sharp angles are fine, as long as the rim doesn't

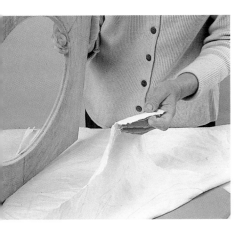

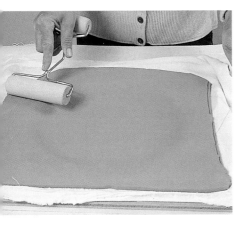

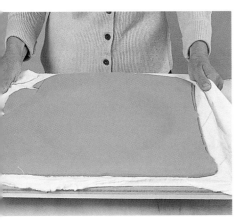

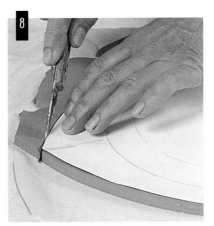

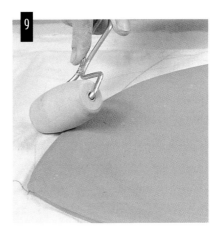

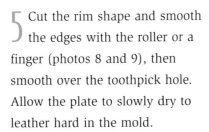

have too wide an overhang. Base the width of the overhang on your clay, the thickness of your slab, and whether or not you want the rim to remain flat and level after it's fired. Different kinds of clay will have different propensities to warp or not warp in drying and firing. Underfiring just slightly or using a thicker slab may help remedy the problem of warping. Wide overhangs have a tendency to slump in the firing, especially if the clay is fired to its vitrification point.

Tip

If you want the rim of your plate to have an even width, before cutting it you'll need to center the template. To do so easily, position a toothpick upright in the center of the plate. Punch a hole in the center of your template, put the template in position over the toothpick, and lightly mark the edges of the template (photo 6). Check to make sure you've marked an even rim before you cut (photo 7).

5 Cut the rim shape and smooth the edges with the roller or a finger (photos 8 and 9), then smooth over the toothpick hole. Allow the plate to slowly dry to leather hard in the mold.

6 For the two smaller plates, use slabs measuring approximately

14 x 14 inches (35 x 35 cm) and 11 x 11 inches (27.5 x 27.5 cm) and ¼ inch (6 mm) thick. The slab for the platter should measure approximately 16 x 23 inches (40 x 58.4 cm). It's a good idea to measure the inside dimensions of your kiln before finalizing the size of your platter, just to make

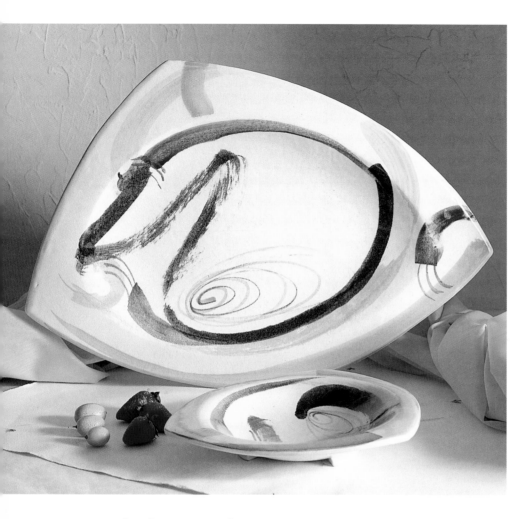

prevent warping that could occur if you picked up the pieces by the rims and flipped them over. Out of the leather-hard slab, cut shapes for the feet. (Placing three feet on each piece will help make your pieces level and prevent rocking.) Score the feet and the bottoms of the pieces, apply slip, and join the feet and the pieces (photo 10), tapping the joins with a wooden paddle to firm them. If your platter is particularly large, you may want to use a thicker slab for its feet to make them better proportioned.

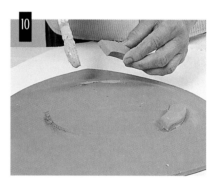

sure the platter you're planning to make will fit. If you want to make the largest platter possible, remember that half the shrinkage in the clay will occur as it dries, so you'll have something slightly smaller than you started with to fit inside the kiln.

7 The slab for the bowl should be approximately 14 inches (35 cm) square and a slightly thicker ³⁄₈ inch (9 mm). A softer or wetter slab may slump more easily (if some of your clay is a little wetter, use it), and a stretchy fabric between the clay and the mold will best facilitate the added slumping necessary to create this

deeper piece. Making the bowl will also require more tapping of the mold. Turn it and tap on each edge until the clay slumps enough. Make sure you carefully center the clay over the hole in the mold, so enough margin of clay remains all the way around the hole for the rim.

8 Roll out a slab about 12 inches (30 cm) square and ¹⁄₄ inch (6 mm) thick for the feet, and allow it to dry to leather hard. After the plates, platter, and bowl have stiffened, lay a ware board on top of each piece and turn each over. The board is important to use here; it helps

9 Let the pieces dry slowly. I found that some warpage can occur in the drying process, but putting the plates back in the molds to dry made them less prone to it. Another helpful trick is to dry the plates upside down while weighing down the rims with pieces of clay weighing approximately ¹⁄₄ pound (112 g). You don't want the weights to be so heavy that the plate rims can't move to shrink.

CREAMER AND SUGAR DISH STEPS

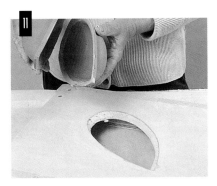

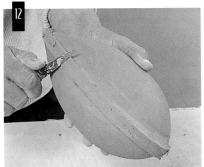

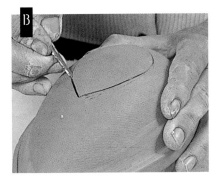

1 Choose a shape and make the mold for the two dishes. You can use one mold, such as the teardrop-shaped mold shown in photo 11, for both. To make the sugar bowl, slump two slabs, each ³⁄₈ inch (9 mm) thick. Allow the two slumped pieces to dry to the same leather-hard stage. You can leave a small rim around the edge of each piece or not. Score the edges, apply slip, join the two pieces, and smooth the join with a knife (photo 12).

2 With a sharp knife held at an angle, cut out an opening on top of the bowl for the lid, and remove the piece (photos 13 and 14).

3 Form a flange for the lid with a coil or slab (photo 15).

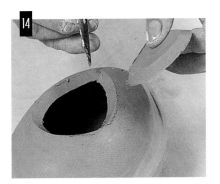

4 Consider where the glazed edge will end at the juncture of the lid and the bowl. You may want to mark a line at this point, to make the glazing look neater. I used a dressmaking tool to scribe a line about ¹⁄₈ inch (3 mm) from

the edge of the lid opening (photo 16).

5 Place the lid back on the pot to make sure it's a good fit, without too much play. Good-fitting lids are a sign of good craftsmanship and one of the first things customers check when they encounter a lidded container. (Putting a piece of thin plastic wrap over the opening before placing the lid back on makes the lid easier to remove until it's dry.) Scribe a line on the lid, just as you did on the bowl in step 4 (photo 17).

6 The fun part for me always comes with the handle design. Try coils, textured shapes, and combinations of different shapes of slabs. You may even want to make a wooden handle later. If so, design a way to attach it now. I decided to simply use a few squished, rounded wads of overlapping clay (photo 18) for the knob on this piece, scoring and applying slip to attach them.

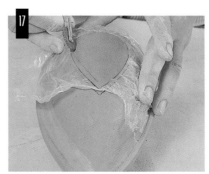

7 The feet for this bowl are made from the same squished, rounded wads of clay as the handle. Remove the lid temporarily. On the bottom of the bowl, score the places where feet will go, apply slip, and add the feet (photo 19). Make sure the piece sits level. When designing feet, consider how the piece will be glazed later. Does the piece sit

high enough off the table so that the glazed belly will not stick to the kiln shelf? Feet are not the only option of course. You could make a foot rim, or you could simply flatten the piece on the bottom. If you decide on a flattened bottom, you'll want to actually make it slightly concave, to prevent the piece from rocking. Once you've added the feet, set the lid back in place.

8 Refer to step 1 to make the base vessel for the creamer, add feet, following the instructions in step 7, then cut out a triangular shape for the spout (photo 20). Texturize this piece, if you like.

9 Scribe and carve out an opening in the pot (photo 21).

10 Attach the curved triangular slab around the opening by scoring and applying slip (photo 22). Paddle the join to strengthen it (photo 23)

11 Squish a button of clay onto the spot on each side where the spout meets the body of the creamer (photo 24).

12 With your finger and water, gently form a lip on the end of the spout to facilitate pouring (photo 25). Just as with the pitcher and teapot spouts in Chapters 2 and 4, carefully consider the angle of the edge of the

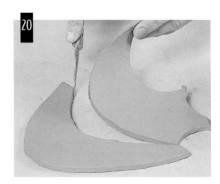

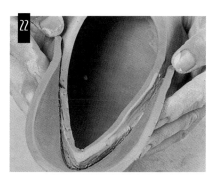

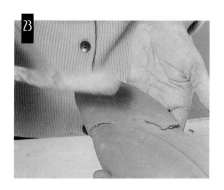

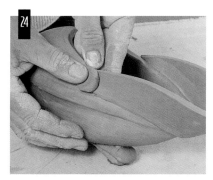

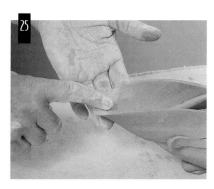

spout so that it creates a good, nondribbling pour.

13 Make any sort of handle you like out of a coil or slab of clay, and attach it after scoring and applying slip. The section on cups for this setting (page 100) includes instructions for making many different handle variations. Here, I'm making what's known as a pulled handle, a longtime top choice of potters for both strength and flowing lines. With an elongated lump of clay in one hand, start pulling with the other hand, using slip or water to keep the clay slippery, gradually elongating the clay into a ribbon form (see photo 26). This method seems to automatically make a handle that is thicker on one end, and nice and smooth. It is easy to form ridges with a finger. The handle also curves easily into the shape you want without cracking.

14 Allow the handle to stiffen somewhat in the curved form before cutting it off from the lump that's left, then scoring the handle and the creamer and applying slip to attach it (photo 27). It's possible to pull a long ribbon to make a number of handles in one session. With some practice, you can attach a lump of clay directly onto a leather-hard cup, hold the cup in one hand, and pull a handle with the other. This technique encourages a smooth transition between the handle and the cup.

LADLE STEPS

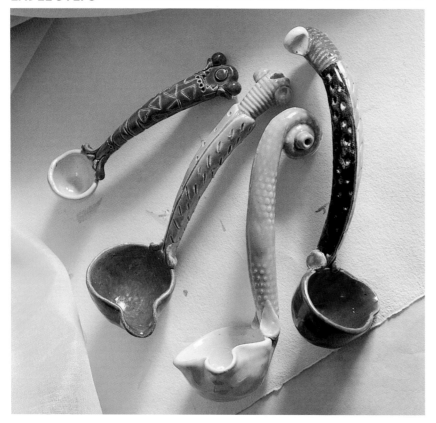

Add a ladle, and the creamer becomes a gravy boat—or a dish for sauce or salad dressing.

1 Pinch a small cup out of a ball of clay, and form a tiny spout on the cup (photo 28).

2 Roll out a coil for the handle, and texturize it, if you like (photo 29).

3 Score the handle and the cup, apply slip, and attach the handle to the cup of the ladle (photo 30).

CUP STEPS

1 Find a form that matches the diameter you want for the inside of the cup. Cardboard mailing tubes (which come in various sizes) work well. So do wooden dowels. Cover the form with a sheet of newspaper to keep the clay from sticking to it, but don't wrap the paper too tight. Roll out a slab about ³⁄₁₆ inch (5 mm) thick. Cut out a piece the height you want the cup and long enough to

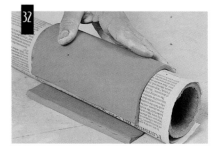

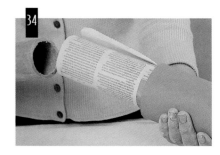

wrap around the tube, with a bit of an overlap. Bevel the edges as you cut the piece (photo 31).

2 Form the piece around the tube (photo 32), roll it along a piece of string to make interesting score lines (photo 33), and press the edges together by pressing the tube onto the work surface. (Because you're working with soft clay, you don't need to score and apply slip to join the edges here.)

3 Carefully slide the clay and paper off the tube (photo 34), remove the paper, and allow the piece to stiffen just slightly.

4 Meanwhile roll out a slab for the bottom that is about the same thickness as the cup. Place the cup on the slab and cut a circle ¼ inch (6 mm) larger than the cup base. With a dowel, thin the

edge of the circle (photo 35), then apply it to the base and use the wooden paddle to fold and press the excess clay onto the base. Another option for attaching the circular bottom to the cup is to cut a circle that is the same diameter as the cup, wait until the circle and the cup are leather hard, then join the two pieces by scoring and applying slip. I chose working with the clay in the softer stage, as it seems to produce an object more consistent with the soft-slab curves of the plates and bowl.

5 Use a long-handled stiff brush to put a small amount of clay slip into the seams on the inside of the cup, filling any crevices. Smooth the rim of the cup, and roll the piece to strengthen all the joins (photos 36 and 37).

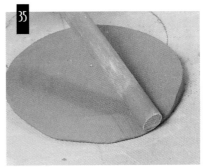

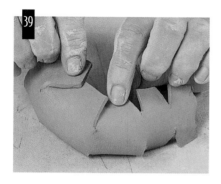

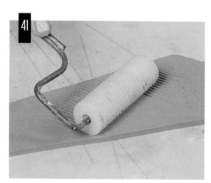

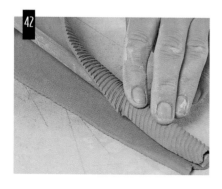

The possibilities for cup handles are limited only by your imagination. Just try to keep in mind how the edges of the handle will feel in your hand and how the proportion works with the cup size. Do you want to put more than one finger through the handle? Do you want to prevent a finger from resting on a hot cup? Will the handle be glazed or unglazed? Will it look (and be) strong enough to hold the filled cup? Will it feel balanced? Will the design be compatible with the design of the rest of the place setting? Here are just a few options.

The Darted Handle

1 Roll out a thin ($\frac{1}{16}$ inch [1.5 mm]) slab and cut out a wedge shape. Cut out several triangular shapes from each side of the wedge (photo 38).

2 Curve the slab by overlapping the edges of the cutouts, pressing the sides gently together (photo 39). Overlap and join the long edges to form a curved tube (photo 40). Practice will show you how the placement of the cutouts can vary the shape of the handle. This form will have a crisper appearance if the clay is not overworked but handled very gently. Allow the handle to stiffen slightly before scoring it and the cup and applying slip to attach it to the cup. Put a small hole in it with a needle tool before firing it, since there may be trapped air inside.

The Squashed, Textured Tube Handle

I learned this one from potter Lana Wilson, and use variations of it often.

1 Roll out a thin ($\frac{1}{16}$ inch [1.5 mm]) slab, cut out a wedge shape, and either press a texture into it or press the slab onto a textured material (photo 41).

2 Using a small wooden dowel to help guide the clay, roll the clay into a hollow tube, pressing the edges gently together, so as not to mar the texture (photo 42).

3 Curve the tube. Occasionally, it will crack if it is curved too much, so be prepared to make another one. Finally, drop the handle on your work surface to barely flatten it (photo 43). Allow it to stiffen before scoring and applying slip to join it to the cup. Put a small hole in it with the needle tool, since it has trapped air inside.

The Ribbon Handle

Roll out a slab about $\frac{1}{4}$ inch (6 mm) thick, and cut out a strip. Use a tool or a finger to make ridges in the strip lengthwise (photo 44). I personally find this a more appealing handle if the shape varies in width or thickness. Also, make sure the edges are not sharp, but rounded. Use a damp sponge to smooth the edges. For a variation, try rolling

one end of the strip into a coil before scoring and applying slip to attach it. Oftentimes, I see this type of handle erring on the side of thinness, which gives it a dangerously fragile appearance (and indeed makes it fragile), so beware of this pitfall.

The Coil Handle

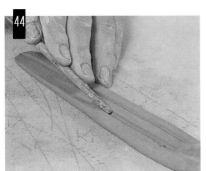

Roll out a coil (photo 45), texturize it if you like (photo 46), and score and apply slip to attach it to the cup. Think about the joined area in terms of both strength and glazing possibilities. A small coil wrapped around the handle and cup juncture can lend a delicate touch and strengthen the join. Do you want the handle to be glazed a different color from the cup? If so, a line on the cup or on the coil could make that color division crisper and perhaps easier to execute.

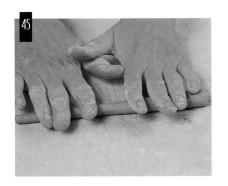

The Slab Handle

We made a slab handle in Chapter 4, but here I've made it with a cookie cutter (photo 47) and also added a small strip to the design to act as a finger rest (photo 48).

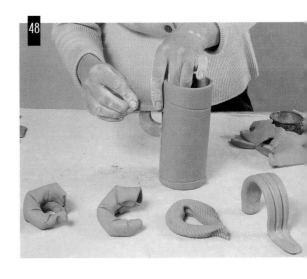

The Pulled Handle

This is the handle we added to this setting's creamer. See page 99.

Before joining handles and cups, try to make sure the pieces have matching moisture contents, making a crack in the join between the two less likely. You can wrap the handle with plastic to prevent it from drying faster than the cup.

After all the pieces have slowly dried, bisque fire them.

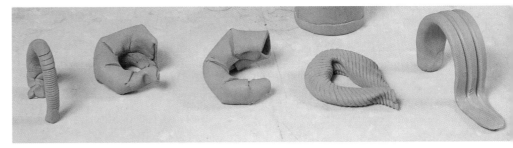

GLAZING STEPS

Y ou can find underglazes in a huge range of colors, or you can mix your own. You can also purchase them in pencil, crayon, chalk and numerous other forms. Choose your underglaze colors and test them first under the clear glaze. The colors of underglazes in purchased bottles and of underglazes that you mix yourself will be similar to but not always identical to their fired colors. Sometimes, the colors will change slightly because of the types of ingredients that make up the glaze. Try overlapping colors, mixing colors, and using thick and thin applications of colors to learn about the range of possibilities. Also, try out different brushes and other application methods, such as using a sponge, to apply the underglaze. Try cutting or tearing shapes out of newspaper, wetting the shapes, laying them on a bisque-fired form, and then painting or spraying the underglaze over this stencil. Try wax resist between layers of underglazes, burning it off in the kiln before the glaze coat.

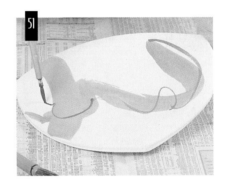

Making flowing, spontaneous, elegant brush strokes is an art in itself. It helps to practice for a long time on paper to learn to make them without hesitation or a heavy, clumsy feel. Good brushes in different sizes are essential, and you may find that

making your own leads to new ways of manipulating the underglazes. Some potters use ordinary foam brushes, but cut them to create special strokes. You could also use a slip trailing bottle or an ear syringe to apply the colors in dots or lines.

Tip

If you apply the underglazes too thickly (i.e., too many layers of overlapping colors), the glaze may bubble over them.

1 After you have practiced application styles and tested your color(s) under a glaze through a firing, prepare the bisque-fired pieces for glazing. Brush off any dust. If there are rough spots that you overlooked, use sandpaper to smooth them. Check the insides of the containers for any small shards.

2 With a brush, paint wax resist onto any areas that will come into contact with or be close to the kiln shelf. Allow the wax to dry. Apply the underglazes in the style you have chosen (photos 49 through 51). If you make a mistake, just wash the piece off with water, allow it to dry, and start over.

3 Always wear a respirator when spraying glazes, and spray them in a properly ventilated spray booth (photo 52). Handle the pieces with care, so as not to smear the decoration. Spray the clear glaze on the bottom of each piece first. Once it dries (which happens quickly), turn the pieces over and spray the top sides. Before spraying the outsides of the cups, pour glaze into them and pour it back out, to glaze the insides.

Experience will tell you when the glaze coating is thick enough. Usually, you will spray until the underglaze design is no longer visible, but you should try one piece as a test first. Refer to page 48 for more information on glaze application with a sprayer. If you don't have a setup for spraying, you can mix a larger quantity of glaze and dip the pieces. For dipping an entire piece at one time, glaze tongs come in handy, though you may need to use a brush to touch up the tiny unglazed spots they can leave behind.

4 The sprayed glaze coating is very fragile, so handle the pieces carefully as you wipe the feet with a damp sponge to remove any glaze that accumulated there. Use a brush and extra glaze to touch up any areas that may have chipped in handling, then load the pieces into the kiln.

5 Fire to Δ4.

Tip

Did any of the rims warp downward in the firing? If so, you may be able to refire these pieces with a small prop called a pointed stilt situated under the drooping area.

> Food presentation
> should always have
> an unexpected element.
> That is, the plate should
> have some design on it—
> a lively surprise—
> not discovered
> until
> the food
> is gone.
>
> Francois Manavit
> Chef
> French cuisine

CHAPTER 6

SURFACE DECORATION STYLES

FOUR ARTISTS AND THEIR STYLES

The techniques for making a slab plate are fairly limited, but the choices for decorating that plate are vast. The four artists who demonstrate their unique surface decoration techniques in this chapter present only a small fraction of the possibilities for surface decoration. None of the four developed his or her particular style right away. Their styles evolved over the years through constant experimentation—through making marks, rejecting some marks, and making small changes. In this way, each artist's style evolved into one that became more personal as the work progressed. On the following pages, they share some of the influences that have inspired their vocabulary of shape and motif and demonstrate how they achieve the effect they want.

SYLVIE GRANATELLI makes functional tableware and seeks to create a special mood or atmosphere, highlighting food with her beautiful serving pieces. Her Sicilian and Cajun roots contribute to her strong affinity for cooking, hospitality, and the ritual of eating. While at the Kansas City Art Institute, she fell in love with Japanese ceramics and English folk pots. Her style has also been influenced by her love of the sensuality of porcelain—the way light gathers in the clay, the way the colors stay bright, and the way it can look liquid, even after it is fired.

Sylvie Granatelli
USING MULTIPLE LAYERS OF UNDERGLAZES WITH GLAZES

Change comes easily to Granatelli (in fact, she says the temptation is to change too much). Her shapes evolve continuously to reflect contemporary cooking trends and eating habits. Her concentration on a particular surface treatment runs in five- to eight-year cycles. Sometimes she returns to old textures and patterns using different techniques. The fruit forms shown here resulted as a way of establishing a contrast between the voluptuousness of the fruit versus the containment of the pottery form. She enjoys making pots for specific functions, and when she sets her own table for a feast, she combines tableware by many potters as well as industrial ceramics, mixing it all up.

Granatelli begins her glazing technique on several greenware platters that have been hump-molded over plaster forms. She prefers to work on several pieces at one sitting, for efficiency. The platters have extruded feet and rims and pulled handles. She has sprayed a thin layer of underglaze on each.

1 She starts by lightly sketching pencil designs on the stain (photo 1).

2 Next, she fills in the sketched shapes by brushing on underglazes of yellow, chartreuse, orange, red, tan-taupe, and differ-ent shades of green (photos 2 and 3). She handles the brushes with a light, gestural touch, overlapping colors and applying them loosely, so that the brush strokes are visible.

3 Using a black underglaze and a small, pointed brush, she outlines the shapes (photo 4).

4 With a cutting nail, which is a thick, wedge-shaped nail, she scratches through the designs (photo 5). The action creates a powdery residue of underglazes and clay body, which she leaves on the surface.

5 After waiting an hour (or overnight), she uses a finger to smudge and blend the residue, which softens the design (photo 6), then she blows off any excess residue.

6 She bisque fires the pieces to Δ04. After firing, she pours a clear glaze on the insides of the pieces to coat the interiors, then pours it out and wipes off the rims, to remove the glaze from those areas. Using a commercial liquid latex resist, she paints over the clear glaze; she also paints the feet of each piece with a liquid wax resist. She then submerges the pieces in a matte glaze to coat the outsides. The matte will form a nice contrast with the clear glaze on the insides. Finally, she peels off the protective latex and fires the pieces in reduction to Δ9 or Δ10.

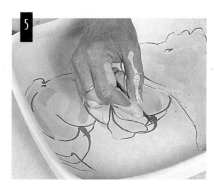

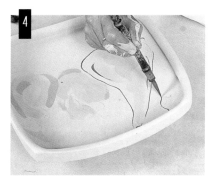

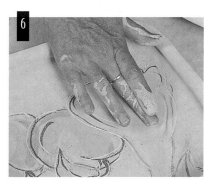

Ken Sedberry
CARVING AND GLAZING GREENWARE

KEN SEDBERRY'S work spans the range from baking dishes and large platters to sinks and sculpture. He takes special interest in the surfaces, making them rich and varied through texture and unusual layers of glazes, combining commercial glazes and underglazes with those he creates and mixes himself. Sometimes the glazes are applied loosely so that the colors merge together, purposefully obscuring some of the imagery. In this way, the motifs are more elusive, not revealed at once, but over a period of time.

Sedberry's travels in Central America have inspired a repertory of animal images: lizards, turtles, snakes, fish, and frogs. He says images sometimes begin to appear that he hadn't anticipated, and only later does he figure out their source. After each piece, he evaluates what works, to his eye, and what doesn't. On the next piece, he concentrates on the successful parts, and through this distillation process, he produces the complex, balanced, and harmonious surface effect he seeks.

Sedberry pounded out 35 to 40 pounds (16 to 18 kg) of a red earthenware, heavily grogged clay (not a slab) over a bisqued clay mold to form the large platter that he will carve. He added a foot rim to the bottom, then once the platter was barely leather hard, he flipped it over onto a bat or ware board. He likes to use bisqued molds rather than plaster ones, because the bisque is so durable and he doesn't have to worry about bits of plaster getting in the clay. The size of his platter (approx-

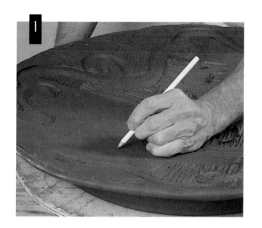

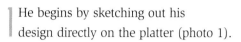

imately 25 inches [63.5 cm] in diameter) is such that he can just fit his hands around it and still fit it into his electric kiln. He also fires in a wood-burning kiln, and plans to fire these platters to the same low temperature in that kiln sometime in the future.

1 He begins by sketching out his design directly on the platter (photo 1).

2 While the clay is still fairly soft, he uses a large loop to carve out the design (photos 2 through 4). He could achieve cleaner details if he waited until the clay was stiffer, but he likes the way the glaze works over the more roughly carved areas. He also adds pieces of clay for additional details in certain areas. As he works, he vacuums out the clay scraps his carving creates.

3 Once the piece is dry, he covers the surface with a black commercial underglaze (photo 5), covering both the top side and below the rim on the bottom.

4 As soon as the underglaze is dry, he paints commercial Δ05 orange and red glazes onto some of the carved areas, usually in three thick coats (photos 6 and 7).

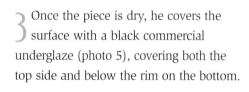

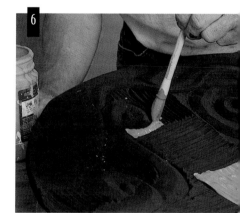

5 He paints the serpent part of his design with a crawl type of glaze (see Appendix D for formula), using several coats (photo 8), then loosely paints other colors of commercial Δ05 glazes on other areas, so the glazes will run together slightly.

He fires the piece to Δ05 in an electric kiln for 12 to 14 hours.

Suze Lindsay
USING SLIPS, PAPER RESIST, AND SGRAFFITO ON GREENWARE

Lindsay decorates her work with bold lines and repetitive designs in an earthy palette of stains, slips, and glazes, never covering the entire piece with glaze. She often combines hand-building with thrown forms, creating animated pieces with distinct personalities and attitudes. Her style has evolved over a decade during which she has made the same forms over and over—but never quite the same. She likes the conversations the pots have when they are grouped together and therefore works on a whole series at once. Despite her vast array of markings, she continues to find new motifs from nature, and rearranges them in different ways. Her goal is to make "good, happy" pots that are works of art, integrated into daily living through use.

SUZE LINDSAY is known for her salt-fired, highly decorated vases, teapots, candelabra, plates, bowls, and cups. She identifies a vast array of historical references as influences: Mimbres pottery from the American southwest, ancient Greek figures from the Cyclades, Japanese 16th-century Oribe ware, and textiles and designs from indigenous cultures around the world. Other important influences are other potters, especially her teachers, and natural objects from her own backyard outside of Penland, North Carolina.

Lindsay handbuilds her forms, using an assortment of bisqued molds to make different clay shapes. She drapes slabs of white stoneware over the molds, puts the shapes together, and then smooths them with ribs. She applies her surface decoration to the leather-hard ware. The pieces are fired once in a salt firing. Here, she works on a candelabra and a salt and pepper set.

1 With a wide, flat brush, Lindsay brushes a white slip on the inside of the base of the candelabra and over the outside of the piece, then uses the brush to smooth over any drippy areas (photo 1). She sets the candelabra aside to dry while she dips the salt and pepper set in the slip, one-third of a piece at a time (photo 2). She shakes the dipped pieces so that drips will not run down the sides, and lets them dry just enough so that they aren't tacky to the touch.

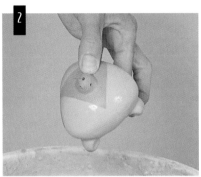

2 She cuts stencils out of newsprint, dips them in clean water, and places them on the upper section of the candelabra (photo 3). With a sponge, she presses the paper shapes, so they lie flat and there are no wrinkles (photo 4). As she works, she overlaps the stencils. If they start to dry too soon and lift off, she sponges them back down or sprays the piece with water.

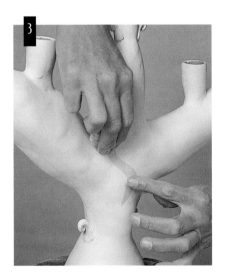

3 Next, she uses a wide brush to paint black slip over the stenciled area (photo 5).

4 One piece of the salt and pepper set receives a spiral paper stencil on all three points with black slip over it (photo 6), and the other piece gets a little spiral brushwork with the black slip (photo 7). It's applied with a deer-tail brush made by Lindsay's husband, potter Kent McLaughlin.

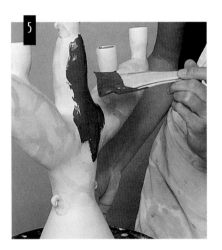

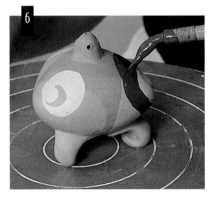

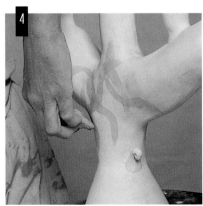

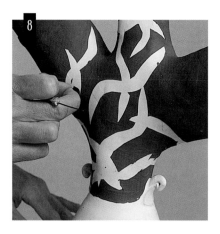

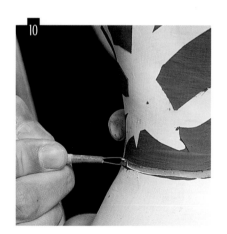

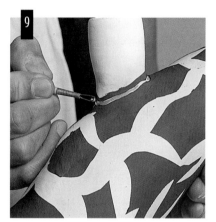

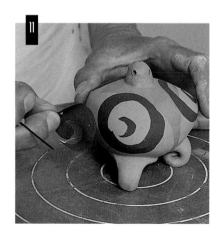

5 She uses her fingers and a fine needle tool to lift off the candelabra stencils when the paper starts to dry (photo 8).

6 She places the candelabra on a turntable and uses a small loop tool to carve a line, sgraffito style, around the base of the candle cups, turning the wheel slowly around as she carves (photo 9). She makes another line around the waist of the candelabra (photo 10).

7 She then peels the stencils off the shaker (photo 11) and makes sgraffito lines around them.

8 Using a pointed brush, she applies black slip around the candle cups, on the curlicues, and around the base. She paints stripes down the base and on the cups (photos 12 through 14).

She lets the pieces dry slowly and then fires them in a gas kiln in a neutral atmosphere for 32 hours to Δ10. She introduces salt at about Δ8 or Δ9.

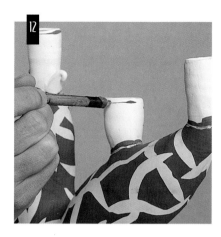

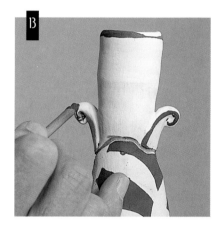

Peter Karner
USING GLAZES AND WAX RESIST

Through trial and error, Karner has developed a palette of glazes that work well in conjunction with each other and with his kiln. His pots are made in a series, so he can note the subtle differences in the details of curve, lip, and foot in an effort to find the form that "sings." His glazing process is accomplished with a boldness and fluidity of motion, so a drip here and there of one glaze on another makes the piece appear spontaneous rather than accidental. He likes making a lot of work, so he's not so attached to one piece and can take more chances in the glazing.

Karner found a wooden bowl that was just the right shape in which to slump a slab to form the kind of ceramic bowl he wanted. Before using it, he sealed the wood and lined the wooden bowl

with newsprint. He used a credit card as a rib to smooth the clay surface in the mold and a needle tool to even the rim. Then he bent the rim, formed it inward, and smoothed it with a chamois. Once the clay was stiff, he removed it from the mold and added two feet to the bottom. He bisque-fired the bowl to Δ06, then applied wax resist to the feet before glazing.

1 First, he dunks the bowl in a bucket of Carbon-Trap Glaze (see Appendix D), up to about halfway, then pours on additional glaze to cover up to about two-thirds of the inside space (see photo 1, page 114). As he works, he tilts the bowl to distribute the excess glaze on the inside and under the lip.

2 Once the piece is dry, he repeats the process, holding the bowl from the

PETER KARNER works in reduction-fired stoneware and porcelain to produce his functional ware. His geometric surface designs make the work stand out as contemporary, while the loose construction provides a handmade sensibility. His work follows in the tradition of many potters before him, but his own way of designing the surface is influenced by the geometric and linear patterns found in the textiles and ancient pottery of Africa, Persia, Japan, and the American Southwest. He is also inspired by the ridgelines of the Colorado mountains outside his studio, as well as by the plants and birds he sees there.

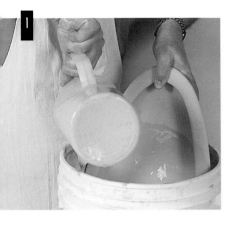

other end (photo 2), then wipes the feet with a sponge (photo 3).

3 With a pointed bamboo brush and wax resist, he begins painting geometric shapes on the inside of the bowl, starting in the middle (photo 4). To make the design less static, he turns the bowl as he works, so the shapes won't all be painted from the same angle. He uses bold strokes, since the next glaze coating may flow and obscure the strokes slightly. The lines are not made with great precision; that is, the brush strokes are loose and fluid, so that a drip here and there won't matter.

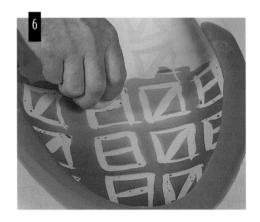

4 Next, he dips the bowl about halfway into a bucket of Green-Black Glaze (see Appendix D), then pours additional glaze onto the inside (photo 5).

5 Quickly, before the glaze dries too much, he carefully sponges off the beads of glaze remaining on the wax (photo 6).

6 He repeats step 4, holding the bowl from the other end (photo 7), and again sponges off any beads of glaze.

7 With a pointed brush, he paints Ohata Khaki Glaze (see Appendix D) in small areas within the geometric patterns (photo 8).

H e fires the glazed piece to Δ9 in a gas kiln in a reduction atmosphere.

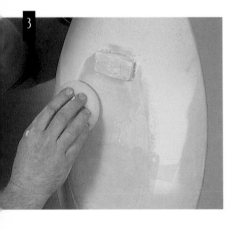

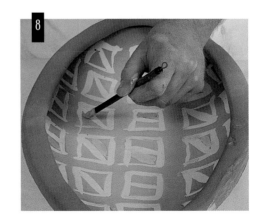

CHAPTER 7

FINDING YOUR STYLE

STUDENTS OFTEN ASK how they can develop a style or "find their voice." It strikes me as an odd and baffling question, as if perhaps their voice has been lost, just slipped away somewhere, maybe down to the bottom of the sock drawer. Typical answers to such questions—to "follow your inner spirit" or to "be in the moment"—all ring true, but we hear them so often they have become clichés, and the meaning doesn't quite hit home.

Carol Gouthro, *Square Platter*, 12" (30.5 cm) square, 1998. Terra-cotta, slump molded over a form; low-fire underglazes, clear glaze, sgraffito; Δ04 bisque, Δ05 glaze. Photo by Roger Schreiber

My answer to how you can find your style may not be the one you want to hear, because it uses the words *exercise* and *work*. But before I get into that, I'd like to ask you to think about how you developed your very own, unique style of handwriting, in spite of the fact that everyone was taught about handwriting in a similar way. There was an inevitability and naturalness to what became your handwriting style, but you had to start with the simple act of practicing forming the letters first, learning a vocabulary of shapes. Then, style evolved on its own. Exercise and work mean you just have to dive in and make something—and practice making those somethings—because you have to first get acquainted with the material and discover what it can and can't do. Don't worry about style when you first start out, but think about structure. (*Will it stand up or roll over?*, for example.) Later, when you can make a predictable form, you can consider the myriad of variations in form and pattern.

In other words, the clay itself will be your first teacher as you begin uncovering your style. You'll learn from clay by working with it yourself—and by paying attention to how others do so. Look at as much work by other artists, both past and present, as you can. Study the different techniques you see, and try to duplicate them. See how it feels to use different brushes, carve through slips with various tools, and fire in different kilns. Don't consider this sort of borrowing or imitating of historical style a bad thing. It's only

Karen W. Sullivan, *Cups*, 4" x 6" (10.2 x 15.2 cm). Stoneware; glazed; fired to Δ11. Photo by artist

Anne M. Koszalka, *Pouring Pot*, 5½" × 2" × 4" (14 × 5.1 × 10.2 cm), 1999. Slab-built earthenware; terra sigillata; Δ04. Photo by Sandi Pierantozzi

plagiarism if you can't move on and put your own spin on it. We don't ever really invent new shapes, we simply find new interpretations of existing ones and new solutions to long-standing challenges. Some theme or technique may attract you at the outset, then, chances are, you'll find someone has already gone in that same direction. But with practice, you will distill out those traces that ring true to you.

If you're feeling that beginner's awkwardness (compounded by the fact that the student next to you or your friend who is also taking up handbuild-

ing is an obvious prodigy), remember that the young genius doesn't always stay ahead of everyone else throughout his or her career. Practice and work can get you to the same level. Watch that prodigy, though, because his or her work may spark some ideas in yourself.

As you practice and work, try *everything*. This approach, even to the point of learning skills that don't have immediate appeal, doesn't mean that you will obliterate your voice. Studying with a strict teacher who focuses only on a particular school or method doesn't necessarily mean the destruction of individual voice, either. Even though Beethoven's compositions often showed the influence of his teacher, Haydn, he still made his work his own personal statement.

In addition to trying everything, *look* at everything, and look closely. As you do, try to decide why something appeals to you, or why not. Learning to

Don McCance, *Untitled*, 5" × 7" × 12" (12.7 × 17.8 × 30.5 cm), 1999. Earthenware, pinch and slab; Δ05. Photo by Bart Kasten

see takes discipline and requires breaking away from habit. Try using a magnifying glass to examine the world of insects. Notice the shapes of spaces between the branches of a tree—the negative spaces between objects rather than the objects themselves. Study the way the lights and darks of a painting are balanced or organized. Listen to music or cicadas, and notice the spaces between the sounds rather than the sounds themselves. Look at work in other media. You might also ask yourself about the sources of inspiration that move you at the deepest level. Is it the geometry of Islamic art, the houses of the Hopi, or photos taken by an electron microscope? Don't worry about why they move you, just study them and see how these interests can play a role in your design. In the end, you may discover why.

In all of these instances, record what you see by keeping a sketchbook. Sometimes, an idea or bit of inspiration recorded in the past pops up as useful years later. Musician and composer Bobby McFerrin says he has to set a goal and a deadline or he won't get anything done, so he comes up with two or three ideas a day and finishes them. He doesn't have to like them, he says, but he does have to finish them, because sometimes he won't like an idea at first, but a month later he'll like it a lot.

Finally, as you practice soaking everything in, detach from judging the new and unfamiliar—the sculpture that shocks or disgusts, the music that sounds cacophonous. Just let it run through you. Later on, you may find that it suddenly starts making sense.

Once you've been exercising and working for awhile, you'll have some pieces to show for it, and your next leap in learning will come from evaluating what you've done. Don't judge your work too much as you make it, but when it's finished, assess it carefully. Critique it mercilessly. *Why is this base awkward? Is it proportioned well? Does it have movement, life, repetition, contrast? Does it express what I had in mind, and why?* And most important of all, to me, *Does it have rhythm?* Mistakes you make can provide valuable lessons, and they can lead you into new arenas. Don't be too quick to pass final judgment on your pieces, though. The abstract painter Richard Diebenkorn would finish a work one day and be sure it was entirely worthless, and the next morning decide it was the best thing he had ever done.

It is very difficult to constructively criticize one piece in isolation, so work on a series. Doing so helps you develop an eye for the subtle differences among pieces. Pick out what works on a piece, reject the awkward parts, and start over. Make a lot of work, and at the

Sandi Pierantozzi, *Tall Candlesticks*, 12" × 4" × 4" (30.5 × 10.2 × 10.2 cm), 1999. Slab-built red earthenware; low-fire glaze; Δ05. Photo by artist

Lisa R. Goldberg, *Untitled*, 9" × 9" × 8½" (22.9 × 22.9 × 21.6 cm), 1999. Slab-built stoneware; iron oxide wash, glazed; Δ10 gas reduction.
Photo by Jerry L. Anthony

Jennie Bireline, *Silk Road Teapot*, 9" × 10¼" × 4" (22.9 × 26 × 10.2 cm), 1997. Earthenware, slab; terra sigillata, burnished gold leaf; Δ04. Photo by Michael Zirkle

same time, don't be afraid to scrap work at any stage. The first in a series will never be as good as the rest, and new work will often help you better see the labored, simple, or incomplete aspects of earlier work. Ask questions such as *Is it too tight? Is the proportion so perfect that there is no possibility for gesture left? Or is it too loose, too floppy, too ambiguous in profile and proportion?* A pot's character and mood will be affected by everything from the way you've handled the clay to how you've applied the glaze.

At the same time that you critique the technical quality of your work, remember that it's easy to get *stuck* on technique. If a piece looks exactly like what you intended, perhaps you should consider side-tripping a little. In other words, trust the unexpected twists and turns that occur during the process. Trust is where true value lies. The pot is going to say something to you, have a conversation with you while you make it. Let it speak and take you in a different direction than you might have intended. The American composer Philip Glass once said we should be less concerned with developing style and more concerned with getting rid of it. Sometimes, our habits become too tight, too restrictive, and the work becomes stuck in a pressure vise. Glass solved this dilemma by putting himself in the most untenable situation he could imagine—composing with India's premier musician, Ravi Shankar—in order to change. Technique can become empty virtuosity—a crutch. Then our work becomes a caricature of itself and

David Crane, *Platter*, 10" × 2" × 18" (25.4 × 5.1 × 45.7 cm), 1999. Stoneware, slab made with drape and hump molds; polychrome glaze resist; Δ10. Photo by Jim McLeod

Lisa R. Goldberg, *Cups*, 5½" × 2" × 2½"
(14 × 5.1 × 6.4 cm), 1999. Stoneware,
slabs textured, darted, altered; glazed;
soda-fired Δ10. Photo by Mel Mittermiller

can't push forward. Sometimes, we have to get outside our normal method of working, return to just pinching pots, create new experiences by changing the scale of our pieces dramatically, and then just play in the studio from time to time. Remember, as sculptor Wendell Castle says in his 10 rules for living, if you're hitting the mark every time, you're standing too close to the target.

If the work becomes boring, ask yourself what it was that got you interested in working with clay in the first place? The solitude? The slippery feel of it? Where did that early attraction go? For years, I pushed myself to perfect a precision glazing style of crisply delineated colors combined on one pot. It made the whole glazing process torture. When I finally abandoned it for painting terra-sigillatas using a wide brush, life was so much better, and I suddenly welcomed glazing time instead of dreading it. Just because you adore the look of a particular style doesn't mean you have to adopt that style. You must accommodate your work habits and your personality. Become a collector, if

you can, of others' work in the style you admire, and make yourself happy that way. Or, master a technique you appreciate on one small part of your pieces rather than pulling your hair out over using the technique all day long.

Style is truly an inevitability. Your early pieces may give you only a glimpse of your natural proclivities and the themes you want to tackle, but as you make more and more pots, your signature will emerge as yours, and uniquely yours. The work will take over. All this takes time to brew. But don't wait for the muse to inspire you. The muse is not dependable, only practice is!

Sheryl Zacharia, *Fish Pitcher*, 14½" ×
10½" × 4½" (36.8 × 26.7 × 11.4 cm),
1999. Stoneware, pinched, coiled, paddled; carved, painted with oxides,
glazed; Δ10 reduction. Photo by artist

CHAPTER 8

GALLERY OF HANDBUILT TABLEWARE

A

Shay Amber, *Frida* (butterdish), 4" × 7" × 4" (10.2 × 17.8 × 10.2 cm), 2000. Earthenware, slab and coil; adorned with hand-carved stamps, multiple firings: Δ04 underglaze, fired at Δ04 with luster added, fired again at Δ018. Photo by Neil Pickett

B

Lambeth W. Marshall, *A Spot of Tea,* 14" × 13" × 12" (35.6 × 33 × 30.5 cm), 1999. Slab-built earthenware, slump molds, added coils, extruded spout; underglazes, slips, washes; Δ06. Photo by Jim Kammer & Danny Riggs

C

Georgia Panagiotopoulos, *Leap of Faith,* espresso cup 2½" × 3½" × 2" (6.4 × 8.9 × 5.1 cm), coffee cup 4½" × 6" × 3½" (11.4 × 15.2 × 8.9 cm), 1999. Low-fire white, slab, hand rolled; underglazed, scratched with needle tool; Δ03 bisque, Δ04 glaze. Photo by artist

B

A

C

E

Pamela Segers, *Fish of the Tea,* 1-½" × 15" × 5" (31.8 × 38.1 × 12.7 cm), 1999. Slab-built low-fire white clay; airbrushed velvet underglaze; Δ4. Photo by Studio III

F

Chandler Swain, *Minuet,* highest—14" (35.6 cm), widest—4½" (11.4 cm), depth—4" (10.2 cm), 1999. Slab, hand-rolled, stretched, textured porcelain; stained with diluted underglazes, glazes; Δ6 oxidation. Photo by artist

G

Jill Allen, *Salt and Pepper Shakers,* 4½" × 4" × 3½" (11.4 × 10.2 × 8.9 cm), 5½" × 4½" × 3½" (14 × 11.4 × 8.9 cm), 5" × 4" × 3" (12.7 × 10.2 × 7.6 cm), 2000. Stoneware, pinched, clay scooped from interiors, feet added separately; terra sigillata, underglazes, patina (oxide wash), low-fire commercial glazes; Δ04. Photo by Dwayne Shell

F

E

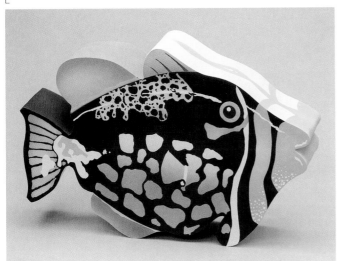

G

A

Linda Arbuckle, *Small Tray: Grey,*
1½" × 6" × 4½" (3.8 × 15 × 11.3 cm),
1999. Terra-cotta, hump mold,
extruded rim and foot; majolica on
terra-cotta; Δ04. Photo by artist

B

Lambeth W. Marshall, *Triangle Server,*
8" × 8" × 6" (20.3 × 20.3 × 15.2 cm),
1999. Earthenware, slab, slump mold;
slips, washes, clear glaze; Δ06.
Photo by Diane Davis

A

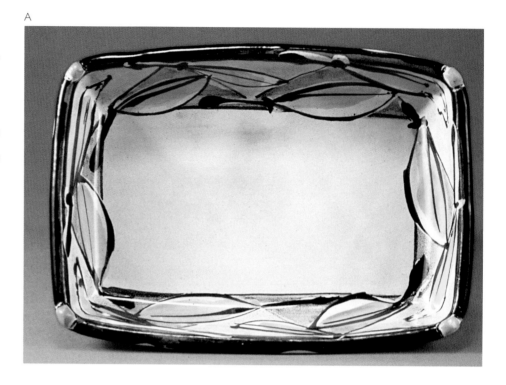

B

C

C
Rosie Souter Paschall, *Spring,* 11" × 14" × 2" (27.9 × 35.6 × 5.1 cm), 1999. Earthenware, hand-rolled slab; carved, glazed, stained; Δ06. Photo by Pro Photo

D
Gail Shaefer, *Fish Platter,* 3" × 20" × 10" (7.6 × 50.8 × 25.4 cm), 2000. Earthenware; hand-painted brush work; Δ04 oxidation. Photo by Diane Amato

E
Rebecca Koop, *Fish and Chips,* platter 17" × 12" (43.2 × 30.5 cm), bowl 7" × 4" (17.8 × 10.2 cm), 1998. Earthenware, slab, hump molds; majolica glaze, stains, oxides; Δ04. Photo by Janet Ryan

F
Carter Hubbard, *Untitled,* 20" × 20" × 3" (50.8 × 50.8 × 7.6 cm), 1998. Earthenware, paper clay, handbuilt; underglaze, clear glaze, gold luster; Δ06, Δ04, Δ018. Photo by Lynn Ruck

D

E

F

A

Natalie R. Kase, *2 Handbuilt Mugs,* 5" × 5½" × 2½" (12.7 × 14 × 6.4 cm), 1999. White stoneware, slab, textured, stretched; dipped in glaze; Δ10 reduction.
Photo by Joseph Qiunta

B

David Crane, *Serving Platter,* 18" × 10" × 2" (45.7 × 25.4 × 5.1 cm), 1999. Stoneware, slab made with drape and hump molds; polychrome glaze resist; Δ10. Photo by Lynn Ruck

C

Carol Gentithes, *Herbivore* (vegetable server), 2½" × 7" × 13" (6.4 × 17.8 × 33 cm), 1996. Earthenware, slab; white slip with alkaline glazes; Δ05.
Photo by Fred D. Johnston

A

B

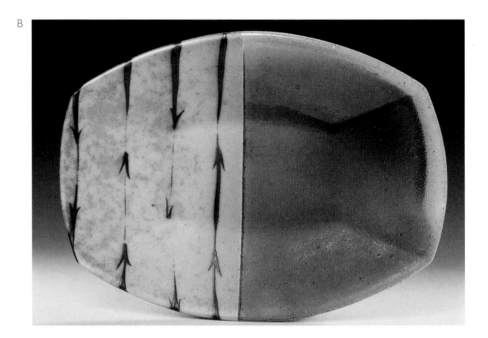

C

D

Ken Sedberry, *Baking Dish and Gratinee,* baker 2½" × 11½" × 16" (6.4 × 29.2 × 40.6 cm) gratinee 1¾" × 7½" × 15" (4.4 × 19.1 × 38.1 cm), 1999. Slab draped over bisqued hump mold, pressed and finished with a rasp and rubber rib; overlapping glazes using latex resist; bisqued to Δ06 electric, wood-fired to Δ10.

E

Carol Gentithes, *Won by a Hare* (soup tureen), 8" × 12" × 16" (20.3 cm × 30.5 cm × 40.6 cm), 1998. Low-fire white-ware, coils and slabs; terra-sigillata applied to textured areas; Δ05, electric.

F

Linda Arbuckle, *Oval Footed Platter: Bud Knobs,* 4" × 20½" × 8" (10.2 × 52.1 × 20.3 cm), 1999. Terra-cotta, hump mold, extruded rim, thrown and altered foot; majolica on terra-cotta; Δ04. Photo by artist

E

F

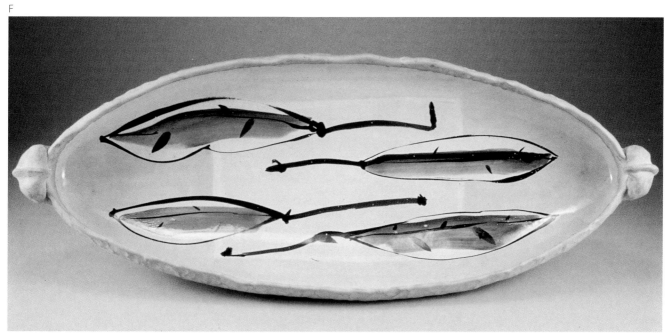

A

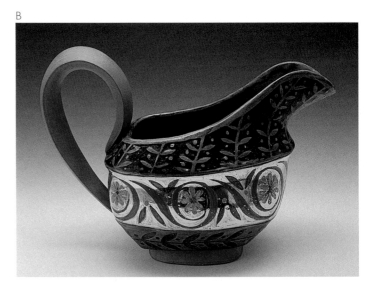

B

C

A
Suze Lindsay, *Tabletop Candlesticks,* 3" × ½" × ½" (7.6 × 1.3 × 1.3 cm), 1999. Slab-built stoneware, feet added; slip and glaze brushwork; Δ10 salt firing. Photo by Tom Mills

B
Erin Furimsky, *Sauce Boat,* 6" × 8" × 5" (15.2 × 20.3 × 12.7 cm), 1999. Earthenware, slab, coiling; terra sigillata, majolica, luster; white slip with carving; bisque Δ04, glaze Δ04, luster Δ18. Photo by Tyler Lotz

C
Suze Lindsay, *Ice Cream Bowls,* 3½" × 5" × 4" (8.9 × 12.7 × 10.2 cm), 1999. Slab-built stoneware with thrown feet; slip with paper resist, sgraffito; Δ10 salt firing. Photo by Tom Mills

D

E

F

D
John Hesselberth, *Tumbler and Juice Cups,*
tumbler 6" × 3" × 3" (15.2 × 7.6 × 7.6 cm),
cups 3½" × 3" × 3" (8.9 × 7.6 × 7.6 cm), 1998.
Stoneware, soft slab; stamped and rolled texture, multiple slips and glazes; Δ6 oxidation.
Photo by artist

E
Anne M. Koszalka, *Covered Jar,* 5¾" × 2" ×
3¼" (14.6 × 5.1 × 8.2 cm), 1999. Slab-built
earthenware; terra sigillata; Δ04. Photo by
Sandi Pierantozzi

F
Marko Fields, *A Teapot for Gaia,* 15" × 16" ×
6" (38.1 × 40.6 × 15.2 cm), 1999. Porcelain,
slab, coil, pinch formed; underglazed, incised;
Δ05 for underglaze, Δ6 oxidations, Δ18 luster.
Photo by artist and Darren Whitley

A

Vicky Conley, *Dragon Plate,*
1" × 9" × 7" (2.5 × 22.9 × 17.8 cm),
1999. Stoneware; embossed from
linoleum cut; Δ10 reduction. Photo by
Doug Conley

B

Bacia Edelman, *Porcelain Ewer,* 10½"
× 9" × 4" (26.7 × 22.9 × 10.2 cm),
1999. Porcelain, rolled slabs;
impressed polystyrene foam net;
reduction salt firing to Δ10. Photo
by artist

C

Laurie Rolland, *Bowl,* 9.5"
(24 cm) tall, 1999. Stoneware, built
in mold, textured; dipped in washes
of two glazes; Δ6 oxidation. Photo
by artist

D

Makoto Hatori, *Oblong Dish with
Legs,* 2¹³⁄₁₆" × 10¹³⁄₁₆ × 8¼ (7 × 27.5
× 21 cm), 1999. Bizen stoneware,
beaten with paddle; traditional
Bizen glaze to 1280 °C (2336 °F)
in oxidized atmosphere, 10-day
firing. Photo by artist

E

Marko Fields, *Pray O Sailor Lost at
Sea, That a Mermaid May Find Thee,*
10" × 15" × 3" (25.4 × 38.1 × 7.6
cm), 1999. Stoneware, slab, carved,
pressed, coiled; underglaze, sponge
wiped; Δ6 oxidation. Photo by artist and
Darren Whitley

A

B

C
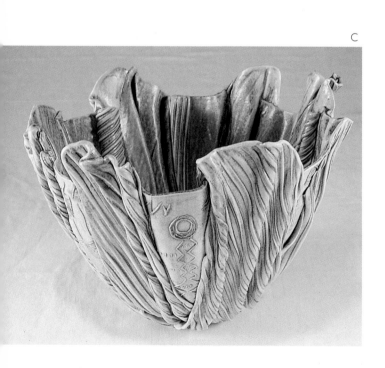

D

E

A
Mary Kay Botkins, *Creamer,* 9" × 5" × 4" (22.9 × 12.7 × 10.2 cm); 1999. Grolleg porcelain, extruded slab, folded handle; glazed; Δ6 oxidation. Photo by Neil Pickett

B
Bryan Hiveley, *Salt and Pepper Shakers,* 4" × 1½" × 1½" (10.2 × 3.8 × 3.8 cm), 2000. Earthenware, slab; sgraffito, glazed; Δ03 electric firing. Photo by artist

C
Robert and Beverly Pillers, *Dinner Plates,* 8" (20.3 cm) and 10" (25.4 cm) in diameter, ¾" (1.9 cm) deep, 1994. Stoneware slab, hump mold; combination of wood ash glazes; Δ11 reduction. Photo by Robert Pillers

A

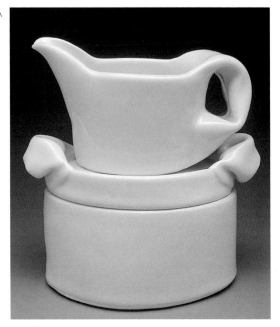

B

C

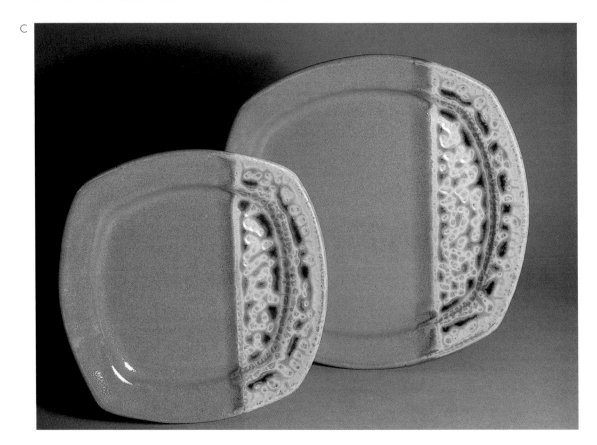

D

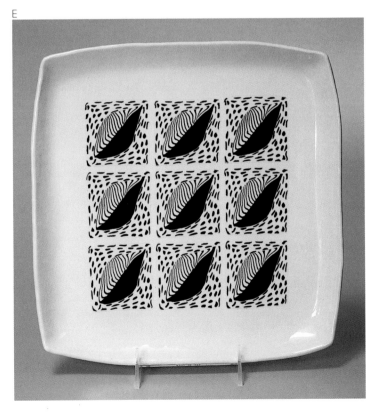

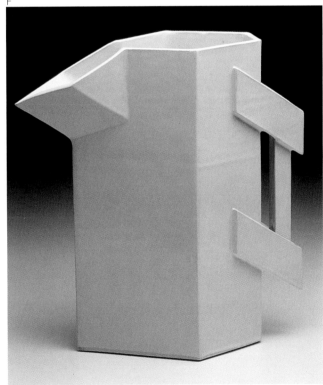

D

Mia Tyson, *Holding Back,* 1½" × 20" × 11½" (3.8 × 50.8 × 29.2 cm); 1999. Thrown disk porcelain, altered with pulled handles; sgraffito (black slip only); Δ10 to Δ11 reduction. Photo by Diane Davis

E

Faith Rahill, *Square Plate,* ¾" × 11½" × 11½" (1.9 × 29.2 × 29.2 cm), 1999. Stoneware, slab with hand-turned edge; neriage; Δ10 gas firing. Photo by artist

F

Kyle Clayton Osvog, *Pitcher,* 13½" × 12½" × 5½" (34.3 × 31.8 × 14 cm), 1997. Slab-built stoneware; high-fire glaze; Δ9. Photo by Wayne Torborg

E

F

A

A

Leslie Green, *Lilies,* 1½" × 8" × ¾"
(3.8 × 20.3 × 1.9 cm), 1" × 6" × ¾"
(2.5 × 15.2 × 1.9 cm), and 2" ×
10½" × 1½" (5.1 × 26.7 × 3.8 cm),
1999. Stoneware, rolled slabs, feet
attached, edges finished with rib
tool and sponge; glazed; Δ6, neutral gas. Photo by Gary Gibson

B

Steve Howell, *Cream and Sugar
Set,* 6" × 8" × 12" (15.2 × 20.3 ×
30.5 cm), 2000. Earthenware,
textured, rolled slabs; decorated
with saturated colored majolica
glazes; Δ03. Photo by Randall Smith

B

D

E

F

D
Sheryl Zacharia, *Tortoise & Hare Sugar & Creamer,* 6" × 12" × 6" (15.2 × 30.5 × 15.2 cm), 1999. Stoneware, slab, pinched, coils, hand-formed animals; carved, underglazed, glazed; Δ10 reduction. Photo by artist

E
Sandi Pierantozzi, *Butter Dish,* 4" × 7" × 4" (10.2 × 17.8 × 10.2 cm), 1999. Slab-built red earthenware, low-fire glaze, Δ05. Photo by artist

F
Mindy Moore, *Dinnerware Place Setting,* dinner plate 13" (33 cm) in diameter; salad plate 5" (12.7 cm) in diameter; bowl 6" × 6" × 2-1/2" (15.2 × 15.2 × 6.4 cm), tumbler 3" × 3" × 7" (7.6 × 7.6 × 17.8 cm), 1999. Slab-built porcelain; drawing in wet slab, glazed; Δ8 oxidation. Photo by Marvin Moore

A

B

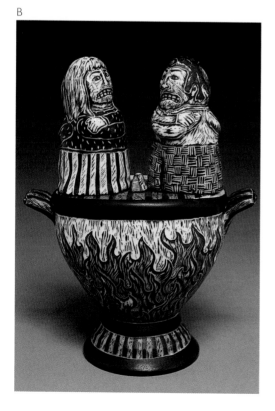

C

D

E

F

A

Kathy King, *Relationship Barometer 1*
Sugar/Salt/Pepper Set, 10" × 6" × 4½"
(25.4 × 15.2 × 11.4 cm), 2000. Porcelain,
shakers handbuilt with press mold, sugar
bowl thrown body, slab lid, handles,
spoon; sgraffito underglaze over clay,
transparent glazes and china paint; Δ6
oxidation. Photo by Charles Mayer

B

Kathy King, *Relationship Barometer 2*
Sugar/Salt/Pepper Set, 7" × 6" × 4½" (17.8
× 15.2 × 11.4 cm), 2000. Porcelain, shakers handbuilt with press mold, sugar
bowl thrown body, slab lid, handles,
spoon; sgraffito underglaze over clay,
transparent glazes and china paint; Δ6
oxidation. Photo by Charles Mayer

C

Chandler Swain, *Larry, Curley, and Moe,*
10" × 6" × 5" (25.4 × 15.2 × 12.7 cm),
1999. Porcelain, slab, stretched, hand-
rolled, textured; glazed; Δ6 oxidation.
Photo by Tim Wickens

D

Nancy Galland, *Live Edge Plate,*
10⅞" × 7½" × ¼" (27.6 × 19.1 ×
.6 cm), 1999. Earthenware, slab, altered
with knife; knife used on edges; Δ10
reduction. Photo and styling by Chiho Kaneko

E

Jenny Mendes, *Two Fine Fellows,* 4½" × 3"
× 3" (11.4 × 7.6 × 7.6 cm), 1999. Terra-
cotta, coil; painted terra sigallatas, layered,
incised; Δ02 to Δ01. Photo by Heather Protz

F

Holly Walker, *Untitled,* 7" × 9" × 6½"
(17.8 × 22.9 × 16.5 cm), 1997. Terra-
cotta, pinched from flattened coils, lid laid
over hump mold; painted glaze and glaze
decoration; Δ04.
Photo by Geoffrey Finkels

G

Marilyn Andrews, *High Wind,* 13" × 12" ×
12" (33 × 30.5 × 30.5 cm), 1999.
Stoneware, coiled from mold, slab relief
additions; slip under clear glaze; Δ5 and
Δ06 oxidation. Photo by John Polak

G

Cone-Firing Ranges

The ranges provided here are for large Orton and Seger cones, fired at a temperature rise of 270°F (132°C) per hour. Note that the temperature at which a cone will melt will vary depending on the rate of temperature rise in your firing.

Orton	Seger	Degrees F	Degrees C
022		1112	605
021		1137	615
020		1175	635
019		1261	683
	019	1265	685
	018	1301	705
018		1323	717
	017	1346	730
017		1377	747
	016	1391	755
	015a	1436	780
016		1458	792
015		1479	804
014		1540	838
013		1566	852
012		1623	884
011		1641	894
010		1661	905
09		1693	923
	09a	1715	935
08	08a	1751	955
	07a	1778	970
07		1784	984
	06a	1803	990
06		1830	999
	05a	1832	1000
	04a	1847	1025
05		1915	1046
	03a	1931	1055
04		1940	1060
	02a	1955	1085
03		2014	1101
	01a	2021	1105
02		2048	1120
	1a	2057	1125
01		2079	1137
	2a	2102	1150
1		2109	1154
2		2124	1162
3		2134	1168
	3a	2138	1170
4		2167	1186
	4a	2183	1195
5		2185	1196
	5a	2219	1215
6		2232	1222
7	6a	2264	1240
	7	2300	1260
8		2305	1263
9	8	2336	1280
	9	2372	1300
10		2381	1305
11		2399	1315
	10	2408	1320
12		2419	1326
	11	2444	1340
13		2455	1346

Kiln Wash Formula

This mixture may be used on kiln shelves (add water and mix to the consistency of cream) or as a dry white, flat underglaze to accentuate texture on dark clay.

Alumina hydrate	65 g
Kaolin	35 g
Bentonite	2 g
	102 g

Magic Water

Use Magic Water like clay slurry for joining slabs of clay.

Add 1 teaspoon of sodium silicate to 1 cup (.24 L) of water

Glaze Formulas

In the glaze formulas that follow, if you measure 1 gram for each percentage point in the basic formula, you'll end up with about ½ cup (.12 L) of glaze. When additional ingredients are listed, the amount to add is given as a percentage of the total weight of the main ingredients.

BLUE SATIN GLAZE

Δ04 to Δ03 Oxidation
(Spicy Harvest Setting, page 50)

Colemanite	39%
Lithium carbonate	9%
Nepheline syenite	5%
Kaolin	5%
Flint	42%
Total	100%

Add ¾% Cobalt Oxide

Variation for rust glaze: add 10% red iron oxide and 10% zircopax

CLEAR GLAZE

Δ4 to Δ5 Oxidation
(Spring Tea Setting, page 76, and
Summer's Bounty Setting, page 90)

Whiting	16%
Frit 3134	16%
Nepheline syenite	24%
Kaolin	16%
Flint	18%
Colemanite	10%
Total	100%

Add 1% bentonite to discourage settling

To color the glaze:

Aqua: 5% aqua-colored green stain

Black: 10% black stain or a mixture of 4% copper carbonate, 4% manganese dioxide, 2% cobalt carbonate, and 4% red iron oxide

Chartreuse: 8% yellow stain and 2% light green stain

Amber: 10% amber-orange stain

Maroon: 8% blackberry stain and 5% deep crimson stain

CHAMELEON GLAZE

Δ5 Oxidation
(Winter Rustic Setting, page 64)

This glaze, which works best on porcelain, is gray when it's thick, tan-green when it's thin.

Soda feldspar	45%
Whiting	10%
Kaolin	20%
Zinc oxide	10%
Talc	15%
Total	100%

Add 3% copper carbonate and 2% lithium carbonate. Hold your glazed pieces at your top glazing temperature for 1 hour, then drop the temperature slowly to 1900°F (1038°C). If the glaze is too dark, refire it.

GRANATELLI'S UNDERGLAZE

Δ9 to Δ10
(Sylvie Granatelli's tableware, page 106)

This glaze works for any temperature on greenware. Equal parts by weight:

> Frit 3110
>
> EPK (kaolin)
>
> Stain

If you're glazing bisqueware, substitute nepheline syenite for the kaolin. Add a few drops of gum solution if the glaze tends to settle.

PATRICK'S LIZARD

Δ06 to Δ04
(Serpent portion of Ken Sedberry's platter, page 108)

Borax	6.3%
Gerstley borate	43.8%
Lithium carbonate	9.4%
Magnesium carbonate	25%
Nepheline syenite	12.5%
Flint	3%
Total	100%

BLACK SLIP

Δ9 to Δ10
**(Suze Lindsay's candelabra and
salt and pepper set, page 110)**

Alberta slip (clay)	78.26%
Ball clay	19.57%
Bentonite	2.17%
Total	100%

Add 7.62% chrome oxide, 1.63% cobalt oxide, and
1.63% red iron oxide.

WILLIE'S 6 TILE SLIP

Δ9 to Δ10
**(Suze Lindsay's candelabra and
salt and pepper set, page 110)**

Nepheline syenite	9.8%
6 tile clay	68.63%
Bentonite	1.96%
Grolleg kaolin	14.71%
Flint	4.9%
Total	100%

Adjust the slip so it's thicker for brushing and thinner for dipping.

EAST CARBON-TRAP GLAZE

Δ9 to Δ10
(Peter Karner's platters, page 113)

Nepheline syenite	50%
EPK (kaolin)	24%
Flint	14%
Whiting	2%
Soda ash	5%
Lithium carbonate	5%
Total	100%

GREEN-BLACK GLAZE

Δ9 to Δ10
(Peter Karner's platters, page 113)

Nepheline Syenite	50%
Flint	28%
Whiting	24%
6 tile clay	14%
Copper carbonate	1%
Copper oxide	5%
Total	122%

OHATA-KHAKI GLAZE

Δ9 to Δ10
(Peter Karner's platters, page 113)

Potash feldspar	35.2%
Flint	16%
EPK (kaolin)	4.4%
Talc	4.4%
Whiting	5.2%
Bone ash	7.2%
Red iron oxide	8%
Total	80.4%

GLOSSARY

Alumina. One of the main ingredients in clay and a refractory ingredient in glazes. Imparts strength to the clay and mattness and viscosity to glazes during firing.

Ball clay. A very fine-grained plastic secondary clay that fires to white or near white.

Bentonite. A very plastic clay added in small amounts to clay bodies to increase their plasticity and to glazes to aid in glaze suspension.

Bisque firing. The first firing of unglazed ware at a low temperature, usually $\Delta010$ to $\Delta05$. Bisque firing removes all moisture from the clay and makes it easier to handle.

Blistering. A bubbled, crater-like surface in a glaze (usually considered a defect) that is caused by too fast a firing or by eruption through the glaze of residual gases in the clay body.

Bloating. The warping, bursting, or bubbling of clay when it undergoes too rapid a firing.

Bone dry. The condition of unfired clay when it is as dry as possible prior to firing.

China paint (or enamel). A low-temperature overglaze fired onto previously fired glazed ware.

Clay body. A mixture of clay and other materials selected to produce particular characteristics to meet the ceramist's needs.

Cones. See Pyrometric cones.

Crawling. Separation of the glaze from the clay during firing. Leaves bare areas. Most often caused by dust or oil on the bisqued ware, too thick a glaze coating, or too rapid a warm-up in the glaze firing.

Crazing. A network of fine cracks in a fired glaze, owing to different rates of expansion and contraction between the glaze and the clay.

Deflocculant. An ingredient of casting slip that reduces the amount of water necessary to make the clay fluid, therefore reducing shrinkage of the slip during drying and firing.

Dunting. The cracking of fired ware during cooling that results from too-rapid lowering of the kiln temperature.

Earthenware. Pottery fired to below $\Delta2$; usually red and porous.

Enamel. See china paint.

Engobe. A type of slip applied to damp or bisqued ware to color its surface.

Flint. Main source of silica in glazes; increases their viscosity and hardness.

Flux. A substance that reduces the melting point of silica in a clay or glaze.

Frit. A glaze that is melted and reground in order to render certain ingredients less toxic. Frits are used as fluxes in glazes and in some clays.

Glaze. A compound of minerals that is applied to the surface of greenware or bisqued ware and that forms a glassy coating when fired.

Glaze fit. Matching a glaze and the shrinkage rate of the particular clay body on which it is to be used. A bad fit may cause the glaze to craze or shiver.

Glaze firing. A kiln firing that reaches temperatures at which glazes will melt. A glaze firing is usually higher than a bisque firing and will usually bring the clay body to its maturation point.

Greenware. Pottery that has not been fired.

Grog. Ground fired clay that is added to a clay body to reduce shrinkage and warpage. Available in different mesh sizes.

High-fire clays. Clays such as stoneware and porcelain, which vitrify at temperatures higher than 2000°F (1093°C).

Hydrometer. An instrument that is dropped gently into a glaze mixture to gauge its thickness.

Kiln. A furnace, built of a refractory material, for firing ceramic ware.

Kiln furniture. Heat-resistant posts, shelves, and other devices upon which ware is supported in a kiln during firing.

Kiln sitter. A kiln mechanism that automatically turns off the kiln when a small pyrometric cone in it slumps.

Kiln wash. A refractory coating applied to kiln shelves to prevent excess glaze from fusing ware to the shelves.

Leather hard. The condition of a clay body that has dried somewhat but can still be carved or joined.

Low-fire clays. Clays such as earthenware, which mature below 2000°F (1093°C).

Luster. A type of metallic coating that is applied to a glazed surface or clay body and fired to a low temperature to give an iridescent sheen.

Majolica (or Maiolica). Spanish surface decoration technique for earthenware in which a tin-opacified glaze is often colorfully painted.

Maturing point (or maturity). The firing temperature and time in firing at which a given clay body reaches maximum hardness or at which a given glaze melts to the desired point.

Overfire. To fire a glaze or clay body beyond its maturation temperature.

Overglaze. A low-temperature glaze that is applied on top of previously glazed and fired work and then fired again. Also called enamels or china paints.

Oxidation firing. A firing with an ample oxygen supply. Electric kilns provide oxidation firings.

Peephole. A hole in a kiln chamber, covered with a removable plug, through which one can observe the pyrometric cones, color, or atmosphere inside the kiln. Welder's goggles should be worn during viewing.

Pony roller. A tool with two wooden dowels, one rounded and one straight, useful for smoothing edges.

Porcelain. Ceramic ware or the clay from which it is made. The fired ware (porcelains are traditionally fired above 2300°F or 1260°C) is very hard, and white and translucent where thin. Lower-fire porcelains have been developed in recent years.

Press mold. A one-piece mold into which clay is pressed or casting slip is poured.

Primary clays. Clays that are found in the ground at their source of origin.

Pyrometer. An instrument for measuring the temperature in a kiln during firing and cooling.

Pyrometric cones. Small, pyramid-shaped forms, made with ceramic materials and formulated to bend and melt at specific temperatures. Used to gauge temperatures in kilns.

Reduction firing. A firing in which the deliberate reduction of oxygen in the kiln results in incomplete combustion of the fuel. This in turn causes carbon monoxide to rob the oxides in clay and glazes of oxygen, thereby causing them to change color.

Resist. A material or method in which a coating such as wax or oil is applied to bisqued or glazed ware to prevent a glaze applied on top of the resist from adhering to the clay or glaze underneath it. The resist burns off during firing.

Salt glazing. A glazing method in which salt is introduced into a hot stoneware kiln, where it forms a glaze on the exterior of the ware. Salt glazing produces toxic fumes.

Secondary clays. Primary clays that have been moved from their source of origin by natural forces such as wind and water.

Sgraffito. A surface decoration technique in which the ceramist scratches through a layer of slip to reveal the clay body underneath.

Shivering. Occurs when a glaze is too compressed, which causes it to separate from the clay and peel or shiver, breaking off in small flakes. This is frequently due to the clay shrinking more than the glaze.

Silica. See Flint.

Slip (or slurry). A mixture of clay and water. Called an engobe when additional materials are added, and called casting slip when a deflocculant is added for fluidity.

Slip trailing. A surface decoration technique in which the ceramist uses a nozzle to apply slip to the ware.

Soaking. Holding the temperature in a kiln at a certain level in order to allow clay and glazes to mature.

Stains. Commercially processed coloring oxides that are used as additives in clay and glazes.

Stilts. Heat-resistant supports used to raise glazed ware above the kiln shelf so that melting glaze won't fuse the ware to the shelf.

Stoneware. A type of clay (or ware made from that clay) that is fired to a temperature above 2100°F (1149°C), causing the body to become dense and vitrified. Buff to brown in color.

Template. A pattern or cutting guide used to shape or cut clay.

Terra-sigillata. A fine, precipitated slip used to coat the surface of ware in order to make it smoother and more impervious.

Undercut. A negative space that creates an overhang in a solid form. When matched with its corresponding positive space, a locking form results. To be avoided when making models for molds.

Underglaze. A material colored with stains or oxides that is usually applied under—but sometimes over—a glaze.

Vitreous. Glasslike; hard, dense, and nonabsorbent.

Ware boards. Scraps of plywood or sheetrock on which you can roll slabs of clay and move them around.

Wedging. Kneading clay by cutting and reforming it in order to expel air and make the clay homogenous.

CONTRIBUTING ARTISTS

SILVIE GRANATELLI is a studio potter living in Floyd, Virginia. Her work has appeared in exhibitions across the country and is housed in the permanent collections of a number of museums, including the Mint Museum in Charlotte, North Carolina, and the Museum of Ceramic Art in Alfred, New York. She travels extensively conducting workshops, and she has served as an instructor in various college ceramics programs. Silvie has written about ceramics for numerous publications, which have also featured photographs of her work, and she was the 1995 recipient of the Virginia Museum Fellowship.

Since 1996, PETER KARNER has operated his studio in Hesperus, Colorado. He has exhibited his work recently at invitational and juried shows, including the Tempe Festival of the Arts, the Albion College Almuni Invitational, and the Evergreen Arts Festival, where he received a second place award in 1999. His work has also appeared at shows sponsored by the Philadelphai Museum of Art and the American Craft Council.

When she's not creating pottery in her Bakersville, North Carolina, studio, SUZE LINDSAY travels around the United States teaching, conducting workshops, and lecturing at colleges, art centers, and craft schools. She has participated in solo and group exhibitions throughout the country and served as a curator and a juror for numerous shows. Suze's work has been featured in a range of publications and is a part of various permanent collections. Her awards include a recent Emerging Artist award from the National Council for the Education of Ceramic Art. Suze is a member of Carolina Designer Craftsmen, Southern Highland Handicraft Guild, Piedmont Craftsmen, Inc., National Council for the Education of Ceramic Art, and American Craft Council.

KEN SEDBERRY has operated his Ken Sedberry Clay Studio in Bakersville, North Carolina, since 1983. Prior to that, he served as an instructor at John C. Campbell Folk School in Brasstown, North Carolina; Penland School of Crafts in Penland, North Carolina; Rhode Island School of Design in Providence, Rhode Island; and various other institutions. He also served as a resident artist and instructor at the Archie Bray Foundation in Helena, Montana. Ken's work has been included in invitational and juried exhibitions throughout the country and has appeared in various national publications. His recent awards include a Merit Award from the Piccolo Spoleto Crafts Show in Charleston, South Carolina. Ken is a member of Southern Highland Handicraft Guild and Piedmont Craftsmen, Inc., and his work is held in several permanent collections, including that of the ambassadorial residence in Niamey, Niger, Africa, through the U.S. State Department's Art in Embassies program.

GALLERY ARTISTS

Jill Allen (page 121), Rock Hill, SC

Shay Amber (pages 41 and 120), Asheville, NC

Marilyn Andrews (pages 35 and 135), Plainfield, NY

Linda Arbuckle (pages 122 and 125), Micanopy, FL

Renee Baltzell (pages 41 and 46), Kansas City, MO

John Berry (page 27), Kent, England

Jennie Bireline (page 118), Bireline Studios, Raleigh, NC

Mary Kay Botkins (cover and pages 22 and 130), Candler, NC

John Britt (page 24), Dys-Functional Pottery, Dallas, TX

Robin Campo and Patricia Guerra (page 43), Norcross, GA

Patrick Timothy Caughy (page 37), Baltimore, MD

Vicki Conley (page 128), Pinon Pottery, Ruidoso Downs, NM

David Crane (pages 5, 118, and 124), Blacksburg, VA

Bacia Edelman (page 128), Madison, WI

Carole Ann Fer (page 39), Cambridge, MA

Marko Fields (pages 42, 127, and 129), Liberal, KS

Erin Furimsky (pages 34, 41, and 126), Rockwood, PA

Nancy Galland (page 134), Live Edge Studio, Stockton Springs, ME

Angela Gallia (page 31), Dallas, TX

Carol Gentithes (pages 124 and 125), Johnston and Gentithes Art Pottery, Seagrove, NY

C. Edgar Gilliam, Jr. (page 12), Roswell, GA

Marta Matray Gloviczki (page 37), Rochester, MN

(continued on page 142)

GALLERY ARTISTS (continued)

Lisa R. Goldberg (pages 36, 117, and 119), Yellow Springs, OH

Carol Gouthro (page 115), Seattle, WA

Leslie Green (page 132), Philomath, OR

Makoto Hatori (page 129), Tamatsukuri-Machi, Japan

John Hesselberth (pages 22 and 127), Frog Pond Pottery, Pocopson, PA

Bryan Hiveley (pages 11 and 130), Gatlinburg, TN

Steve Howell (page 132), Howell Pottery, Gainseville, FL

Carter Hubbard (page 123), Raleigh, NC

Natalie R. Kase (page 124), Sleepy Hollow, NY

Kathy King (pages 42 and 134), E. Walpole, MA

Rebecca A. Koop (pages 22 and 123), Back Door Pottery, Kansas City, MO

Anne M. Koszalka (pages 116 and 127), Philadelphia, PA

Karl Kuhns and Debra Parker-Kuhns (page 29), Parker-Kuhns Pottery, Dolgeville, NY

Suze Lindsay (pages 49 and 126), Bakersville, NC

Molly Lithgo (page 12), Earthworks, Greensboro, NC

Lambeth W. Marshall (pages 120 and 122), Lambeth Pottery, Waxhaw, NC

Don McCance (page 116), Tyrone, GA

Jenny Mendes (pages 37, 42, and 134), Chesterland, OH

Mindy Moore (page 133), Halifax, Nova Scotia

Kyle Clayton Osvog (page 131), Minneapolis, MN

Georgia Panagiotopoulos (page 120), Itchy Dog Productions, Palo Alto, CA

Rosie Souter Paschall (pages 31 and 123), Nashville, TN

Margaret F. Patterson (page 14), Altanta, GA

Rina Peleg (page 46), New York, NY

Sandi Pierantozzi (pages 29, 32, 117, and 133), Philadelphia, PA

Robert and Beverly Pillers (pages 22 and 130), Chesapeake, VA

Peter Pinnell (page 83), Lincoln, NE

Gail Price (page 41), Gail Price Studios, Aspen, CO

Barbara Glynn Prodaniuk (page 45), Truckee, CA

Faith Rahill (page 131), Eugene, OR

Laurie Rolland (pages 16 and 128), Vonzad, British Columbia

Betsy Rosenmiller (pages 14, 32, and 33), Tempe, AZ

Will Ruggles and Douglass Rankin (page 34), Rock Creek Pottery, Bakersville, NC

Gail Schaefer (page 123), Efland, NC

Mouse Scharfemaker (page 32), Denver, CO

Ken Sedberry (page 125), Bakersville, NC

Bonnie Seeman (page 28), Plantation, FL

Pamela Segers (pages 27 and 121), Snellville, GA

Jenny Lou Sherburne (pages 31 and 40), Gulfport, FL

Rosemarie Stadnyk (page 38), North Battleford, Saskatchewan

Kathy Steinsberger (pages 31 and 46), Freewheeling Pottery, Raleigh, NC

Isabella St. John (page 17), Blue Moon Pottery, St. John's, Newfoundland

Karen W. Sullivan (page 115), Claremont, CA

Chandler Swain (pages 121 and 134), Ottawa, Ontario, Canada

Mia Tyson (pages 27 and 131), Mia Tyson Inc., Rock Hill, SC

Holly Walker (page 135), Burnsville, NC

Susan Kay Wechsler (page 45), Susan Wechsler Designs, Chester, NJ

Kristal Wick (page 45), Kristal Wick Studio, Arvada, CO

Sheryl Zacharia (pages 119 and 133), New York, NY

ACKNOWLEDGMENTS

Thanks go to:

My husband, **Jim**, for his love and his encouragement
to tackle this kind of project yet again.

All the wonderful artists who contributed their beautiful photos.
I wish we could have included them all.

My editor, **Paige Gilchrist**, for guiding an inveterate procrastinator
through writing and deadlines. Her extraordinary intelligence, unfailing
cheerfulness, and patience kept me on track.

My art director, **Celia Naranjo**, whose keen eye for detail and
artistic and creative skills made photos come alive.

The four talented artists, **Silvie, Ken, Suze, and Peter,** who
contributed so generously of their time and technical know-how
to lend this book depth and variety.

My first pottery teacher, **Bob Westervelt**, for setting
me on this path many years ago.

The chefs and restauranteurs who shared their creative advice on
tableware and food presentation: **Hector Diaz** of Salsa and Zambra,
Victor Giancola of La Caterina Trattoria and Il Paradiso Steak and Chop
House, **Francois Manavit** of the French Window, **Mark Rosenstein** of
The Market Place, and **Peter Wada** of Heiwa Shokudo,
all in Asheville, North Carolina.

Pete Pinnell, for answering technical questions, and for providing so
much technical information in workshops and in his writings.

Rob Pulleyn, publisher of Lark Books, and **Carol Taylor**, publishing
director, for providing me with the opportunity to write this book.

The photographer, **Dwayne Shell**, for taking beautiful photographs,
traveling a long way to do it, and having a good humor the whole time.

Assistant Editor **Veronika Alice Gunter** and all the diligent staff at
Lark Books who organized photographs and other details so carefully.

INDEX